The 'Earth Summit' Agreements: a guide and assessment

To the memory of David Thomas, an outstanding natural resources editor of the *Financial Times*, who died tragically whilst researching the impacts of the burning oil wells in Kuwait

# The 'Earth Summit' Agreements:
# A Guide and Assessment

An Analysis of the Rio '92
UN Conference on Environment and Development

Michael Grubb
Matthias Koch
Koy Thomson
Abby Munson
Francis Sullivan

Energy and Environmental Programme
The Royal Institute of International Affairs
London

## EARTHSCAN

**Earthscan Publications Ltd, London**

First published in 1993 by
Earthscan Publications Limited, 120 Pentonville Road, London N1 9JN and
The Royal Institute of International Affairs, 10 St James's Square, London SW1Y 4LE

Reprinted 1995

Distributed in North America by
The Brookings Institution, 1775 Massachusetts Avenue, NW,
Washington DC 20036-2188

A catalogue record for this book is available from the British Library

ISBN 1 85383 176 X (paperback)
     1 85383 177 8 (hardback)

The Royal Institute of International Affairs is an independent body which promotes the rigorous study of international questions and does not express opinions of its own. The opinions expressed in this publication are the responsibility of the authors.

Earthscan Publications Limited is an editorially independent subsidiary of Kogan Page Limited and publishes in association with the International Institute of Environment and Development and the World Wide Fund for Nature.

Printed and bound in Great Britain by
Biddles Limited, Guildford and King's Lynn
Cover by Twenty Twenty Design

# Contents

# PART II: THE UNCED AGREEMENTS

# Preface

The UN Conference on Environment and Development (UNCED), popularly known as the Rio Earth Summit, attracted global media coverage and hype. Yet little seems to have happened for example to arrest the growth of greenhouse gases, to alleviate the pressing problems of development and land degradation in Africa, or to protect the forests and biodiversity. Many of the statesmen, politicians and journalists who crowded into Rio have subsequently found other pressing things to occupy their time. To some people, it appeared as a media event and no more.

Yet UNCED was also the culmination of an unprecedented international political process, which attempted to address two immensely difficult tasks simultaneously. It sought to establish a world view of problems of environment and development, including responsibilities for those problems that can only seriously be tackled by international action - action which some countries fear may compromise their sovereignty. At the same time, solutions to these problems require action within national frontiers to look at the processes of economic development in new ways, again something that is easy to talk about but hard to implement. So it is hardly surprising that many conflicts of interest had to be resolved to achieve agreements at Rio, or that the documents themselves are convoluted and often opaque. What is important is that near-global agreement was reached on basic principles, and on follow-up processes that have already been put in place. From this perspective, UNCED was a major step on a long road towards sustainable development, with repercussions ultimately for every business and indeed every individual.

That is why we at Chatham House embarked upon this study of the achievements and implications of the Rio conference. Given the complexity of the process and its products, it is a very ambitious undertaking. But precisely because it is so difficult for even the most interested audience to understand the balance of compromises which led to the resulting texts, and their real meaning, we believe producing a clear and balanced analysis to be a task of particular importance.

Michael Grubb initiated and coordinated the project, and authored Part 1 as well as the chapter on the Climate Convention. Matthias Koch, who spent the summer of 1992 as a visiting student here at Chatham House, is responsible for drafting the Agenda 21 section; Matthias also made important suggestions and provided input into Part 1. As it became obvious that covering the immense range of issues addressed at UNCED would require additional expert input, we were most fortunate to enlist the services of Koy Thomson, Abby Munson and Francis Sullivan as specialist authors on particular agreements, as indicated.

The result is both a reference document, for those who need to refer to and understand the key elements of the agreements reached, and a challenging assessment. I believe the study will be of immense value not just to professionals in the field of environment and development, but to people everywhere with a deep interest in these issues.

Silvan Robinson
Chairman, Steering Committee,
Energy and Environmental Programme,
Royal Institute of International Affairs

Research by the Energy and Environmental Programme is supported by generous contributions of finance and professional advice from the following organisations:

Amerada Hess • Arthur D Little • Ashland Oil • British Coal
British Nuclear Fuels • British Petroleum • Caltex
Chubu Electric Power Co • Commission of the European Communities
Department of Trade and Industry • Department of the Environment
Eastern Electricity • East Midlands Electricity • ELF(UK)
Enterprise Oil • Exxon • GISPRI • Idemitsu
Japan National Oil Corporation • Kuwait Petroleum • LASMO
Mitsubishi Research Institute • Mobil • National Grid
National Power • Neste • Nuclear Electric • Petronal • PowerGen
Shell • Statoil • Texaco • Tokyo Electric Power Co • Total
UK Atomic Energy Authority

# About the authors

**Dr Michael Grubb** is a Senior Research Fellow at the Energy and Environmental Programme of the Royal Institute of International Affairs (RIIA), London. He directed the Institute's international programme on climate change, resulting in a study of the issues and options for negotiating an international agreement on limiting greenhouse gas emissions, and a two-volume international study entitled *Energy Policies and the Greenhouse Effect*. He is an advisor to the United Nations Environment Programme particularly concerning economic aspects of climate change, and to other international research projects on economic and policy aspects of climate change.

**Matthias Koch** studies environmental science at the Technische Universität Berlin, and worked at RIIA for two months on the analysis of UNCED and Agenda 21. His interests focus on international environmental issues and the relationship between scientific and political aspects of environmental protection.

**Koy Thomson** is Programme Director at the International Institute of Environment and Development in London, and author of reports on UNCED and the *Rio Declaration*.

**Abby Munson** is with the Global Security Programme at Cambridge University, UK, where she is conducting research on the use of biotechnology.

**Francis Sullivan** is Forest Conservation Officer at the World Wide Fund for Nature, UK.

## Acknowledgements

This collaborative study was drawn together in a remarkably short time. I am indebted to all the contributing authors for producing excellent studies with such rapidity. Matthias Koch deserves particular thanks for undertaking the immense task of summarising Agenda 21 with great care and dedication, and for offering detailed comments on and assistance with Part 1 of the book. Nicola Steen diligently pursued further attempts to find the real state of financial affairs for Appendix 1.

In addition, I am grateful to all those who attended the study group to discuss the draft text, and to the many others who commented upon it before completion. They have all helped to point out errors and omissions in the drafts, and thus have helped to improve and form the final text. Jackie Roddick of the Scottish Academic Network on Global Environmental Change deserves special thanks for her exceptional efforts in guiding us and providing us with a wealth of background material concerning analysis of the whole UNCED process; and I am deeply indebted to Nitin Desai, the Deputy Secretary-General of UNCED, for reading the full draft manuscript and offering invaluable detailed comments.

Finally, thanks are due to all those on the Energy and Environmental Programme. The former Head of Programme, Dr Gerald Pollio, encouraged the project to expand to a full book, and made valuable suggestions for restructuring the study to make it more accessible. Nicky France edited the text, and Matthew Tickle never faltered in managing the rapid flow of information, requests and comments throughout the project.

Michael Grubb

# Abbreviations

| | |
|---|---|
| UNCED | UN Conference on Environment and Development |
| UNEP | UN Environment Programme |
| UNDP | UN Development Programme |
| UNCTAD | UN Conference on Trade and Development |
| UNCTC | UN Centre on Transnational Corporations |
| (UN)ECOSOC | UN Economic and Social Council |
| (UN)FAO | UN Food and Agricultural Organisation |
| CSD | Commission on Sustainable Development |
| PrepCom | General Preparatory Committee meeting of UNCED |
| IPCC | Intergovernmental Panel on Climate Change |
| GEF | Global Environment Facility |
| OECD | Organisation for Economic Cooperation and Development |
| G77 | Group of '77' (Negotiating group of over 100 developing countries) |
| NGO | Non-Governmental Organisation |
| ODA | Official Development Assistance |

The UN Conference on Environment and Development (UNCED) was the product of a long preparatory history and was unique in its size, scope, level of participation, and process. Most governments submitted reports to the conference on their environment and development outlook, and many established national consultative committees and processes. There was unprecedented involvement from non-governmental groups, and countless national and international conferences on UNCED themes. The UNCED process acted as a catalyst and focus for injecting concepts of sustainable development around the world.

The official product of UNCED resides in five agreements, as summarised overleaf. These establish governing principles and commit governments to a range of post-Rio processes, centred upon the provision of national reports which may be compared internationally and against a limited set of goals established. *Agenda 21* forms the general guideing document for pursuing sustainable development and initiates significant institutional changes. The *Climate Convention* builds in the strongest processes for reporting, review and requirements for amendments to strengthen the regime over time. However, in all the UNCED agreements, specific policy commitments were largely eschewed in favour of further institutional processes, intended to improve understanding and integrated decisionmaking capabilities, and to generate pressures for policy change in all countries.

North-South disputes were endemic in the negotiations, with divisions along axes of relative responsibilities, finance and the control of international financial flows, and the weight given to population or consumption levels as the principle cause of environmental stress. The resulting North-South apartheid reflected in the agreements will remain a central problem in attempts to promote sustainable development, and progress will be slow without more open international discussion of both consumption patterns and population.

Many more specific divisions of national interest were revealed. Some countries used the principle of sovereignty as a way of evading discussion on international responsibilities. The business community successfully pre-empted potential pressures for direct regulation at UNCED by promoting voluntary corporate environmentalism; Agenda 21 emphasises this approach but does not resolve its acknowledged limitations particularly with respect to potential competitive disadvantages and environmental pricing.

Estimates of the financial requirements for implementing each UNCED programme area total roughly to established target levels for Official Development Assistance of 0.7% of GDP. The estimates are of very variable quality, but help to indicate how such amounts might be spent. Available intergovernmental finance remains constant at about half the target level, a constraint which will seriously impede implementation in developing countries and highlight the lack of priorities set by Agenda 21.

UNCED confirmed and enhanced the role of the UN family as the legitimate system for advancing sustainable development. Various non-governmental groups played an important and constructive role, which will be strengthened in the future in both UN and government fora, but this may also make their limitations more apparent. The overall outcome illustrates that popular pressure is only one of many ingredients needed for agreement on substantive policy changes; far more effort is needed to build common understanding of and consensus on the issues, options, and responsibilities.

The UN General Assembly in Autumn 1992 accepted and enacted all the specific recommendations from UNCED. It established the Commission on Sustainable Development (CSD) to oversee the implementation of Agenda 21 in accordance with the terms and principles of other UNCED agreements. Negotiations on a convention to combat desertification are scheduled for completion by mid-1994, and major UN conferences on population and development, migratory fish stocks, and the sustainable development of Small Island States will be held by then. Annual meetings of the CSD will focus on different themes and, with Ministerial level participation, may become a worldwide focal point for review of progress towards sustainable development. The CSD is to complete a 'first round' of review by 1997, when a special session of the UN will review overall progress. The Climate Convention commits Parties to a second major review of progress by 1998.

The international process established by UNCED will ingrain the concept of sustainable development into the UN system, with Agenda 21 as a focus. The goal of sustainable development is here to stay; the most pervasive international tensions in its implementation will be those along the North-South axis, and between the system of agreed UN processes and the shorter-term interests of individual states.

# Box 1: The UNCED Agreements

The **Framework Convention on Climate Change** establishes principles that climate change is a serious problem; that action cannot wait upon the resolution of scientific uncertainties; that developed countries should take the lead; and, that they should compensate developing countries for any additional costs incurred in taking measures under the Convention. The Convention lacks binding policy commitments but indicates that industrialised countries should aim as a first step to return greenhouse gas emissions to 1990 levels by 2000. It establishes a strong process by which governments must submit reports on their relevant policies and projections, and meet regularly to evaluate progress and if necessary amend the commitments. The Convention will enter into force with unusual rapidity.

The **Convention on Biological Diversity** aims to preserve the biological diversity of the planet, through the protection of species and ecosystems, and to establish terms for the associated uses of biological resources and technology. It affirms that states have 'sovereign rights' over biological resources on their territory, the fruits of which should, however, be shared in a 'fair and equitable' way on 'mutually agreed terms'. Countries must develop plans to protect biodiversity and submit some information on them. The Convention may enter into force rapidly, but key developed countries may delay or refuse to ratify it primarily because of concerns over control of funding.

**Agenda 21** is an immense document of 40 chapters outlining an 'action plan' for sustainable development, covering a wide range of specific natural resources and the role of different groups, as well as issues of social and economic development and implementation. It effectively integrates environment and development concerns; it is strongly oriented towards 'bottom-up', participatory and community-based approaches in many areas, including population policy; and it shows more acceptance of market principles, within appropriate regulatory frameworks, than previous UN agreements. Performance targets are mostly limited to those previously agreed elsewhere. Agenda 21 will form the key intergovernmental guiding and reference document on the issues for the rest of the decade.

**The Rio Declaration** comprises 27 principles for guiding action on environment and development. Many address development concerns, stressing the right to and need for development and poverty alleviation. Principles concerning trade and environment are ambiguous and in some tension; others concern the rights and roles of special groups.

The **Forest Principles** form the rump of blocked attempts to negotiate a convention on forests. It emphasises the sovereign right to exploit forest resources along with various general principles of forest protection and management.

# PART I: OVERVIEW

# Chapter 1

## Introduction

The United Nations Conference on Environment and Development (UNCED) in Rio de Janeiro, June 1992, was a unique event in the annals of international affairs. The 'Earth Summit' brought more heads of state and government together than any previous meeting - well over 100, with a 178 governments represented in all. Five separate agreements were signed by most of the participating governments. Thirty thousand people descended upon the city, and the Summit received a blaze of publicity around the world.

In addition to the intergovernmental conference, over 500 different groups with special concerns and expertise on environment and development issues gathered at the parallel Global Forum in Rio, with intensive debate and discussion on wide range ranging issues around the central theme, often including officials from the governmental conference. A major ECOTECH forum and exhibition presented and discussed issues surrounding environmental technology, and dozens of other special events and exhibitions were held around the city.

Yet despite the vast effort devoted to it, and the unprecedented press coverage which it received, to many the Earth Summit is still a mystery. Publicity value apart, the outcome of the Earth Summit has been labelled as everything from a disastrous fiasco to an outstanding success. Which was it; indeed, what was it? What came out of it? What was actually agreed, and what does it mean for the future of environment and development issues?

This report does not attempt to be a comprehensive guide to UNCED; such a task may be impossible, because the enterprise was so huge and complex.[1] Rather, following a short introduction to the origins of and build-up to the UNCED conference in the next chapter, this report focuses upon the official agreements signed at Rio, and the themes and lessons which emerge both from them and the negotiating process. The study highlights the more important areas and offers preliminary observations on important themes and their possible implications for the future development of environment and development issues. The general conclusions from the study, and some observations on prospects for the follow-up process, are presented in Part I. Part II then summarises and examines the individual agreements, including a short review of the processes which led to them, and their likely implications.

---

[1] For sources of the full texts and further information, see Appendix 2.

In this study, we do not seek to analyse in depth all the technical, legal and political aspects of each agreement, which are too complex and varied for a report of this nature. Nor do we examine the many non-governmental activities and publications associated with the conference (including the 'Alternative Conventions' negotiated among environment and development groups), except in so far as they bear directly upon the governmental texts or may have other important ramifications for future developments. Rather, the primary purpose is to give the reader a reference to the official agreements and understanding of their nature and main contents, and to highlight some of the central themes to emerge from the conference and negotiating process as they may bear upon the prospects for follow-up. In doing so, we seek to convey a broad understanding of the central business and legacy of UNCED.

# Chapter 2

## The Road to Rio

## 2.1 Introduction

Concern about the state of the natural environment has deep historical roots, but the nature and scale of concerns, and their political importance, has grown and changed considerably since the wave of environmental protests which swept across developed countries during the 1960s.[1] These debates were directed primarily at local and occasionally regional problems; none appeared to exist at the global level. The lead issues primarily concerned toxic and chemical pollution, such as pesticides, issues which helped to launch the modern environmental movements.[2] Other local problems, such as urban air pollution, were often addressed either by technical fixes to clean up emissions and where necessary dump the residues, or by transferring pollutants into less critical environmental media or by spreading them over a wider area (eg. the 'high chimney policy' adopted to disperse stack emissions). Regulations for some environmental media were developed, but different areas were generally considered separately with little attention paid to their interrelation and interaction. Many years later, limitations to waste dumping, and the potentially devastating effects of the steady accumulation of pollutants in the biosphere became recognised, eg. the acidification of woodlands and lakes, and development of the Antarctic 'ozone hole' and broader ozone depletion.[3]

International agreements addressing environmental concerns are also nothing new. Specific agreements on the protection of particular species, especially migratory birds, date back to well before the First World War. The international

---

[1] For an analysis of the development of environmental concerns on the international agenda, see Caroline Thomas, *The Environment in International Relations*, The Royal Institute of International Affairs, London, 1992, Chapter 2.

[2] Notably, Rachel Carson, *Silent Spring*, H.Hamilton, London, 1963.

[3] The 'ozone hole' is a large area, now expanding out beyond Antarctica to southern parts of Latin America, Australia and New Zealand, in which a rapid and extensive destruction of ozone in the upper atmosphere occurs every spring. The reactions involved are complex and depend upon the very low temperatures in this region, but human emissions of chloroflourocarbon gases (CFCs) are clearly implicated. The 'ozone hole' was an entirely unexpected phenomena; scientists partially understood the underlying reactions, but had overlooked the potential for very cold ice crystals to 'catalyse' destruction at a very much faster rate than predicted. Moderate but accelerating loss of ozone over the Arctic has also been observed, and the global ozone layer is now declining in part because of the destruction at the poles, adding further to perceptions and fears about major, uncontrollable and unpredictable impacts of human activities on the planetary system. Future global warming at the surface, at the expense of cooling in the upper atmosphere, is expected to exacerbate the problem.

Maritime Organisation sought guidelines to address ocean pollution in the 1950s. There was, however, little attempt to address underlying issues of environmental quality in any coherent way until the early 1970s.

## 2.2 The Stockholm Conference

In 1968, at the prompting largely of the Swedish ambassador to the UN, the UN Economic and Social Council (ECOSOC) issued a call which led directly to the UN Conference on the Human Environment at Stockholm in 1972.[4]

Environmental concern in developed countries, particularly the acidification of Scandinavian aquatic systems, was the major factor which led to the Stockholm Conference. During the preparatory work, the emphasis on pollution shifted towards including concerns of developing countries. Initially, many developing countries considered environmental protection as a luxury to be addressed when developmental issues were solved, and were wary of the planned conference. A meeting of experts convened at Founex in Switzerland in 1971 claimed to result in 'the first comprehensive document on the development-environment issue', and helped to produce a more sophisticated view than simple fear of environmental constraints as an impediment to development;[5] anticipating UNCED debates, it '... identified environment as a critical dimension of successful development'.[6]   Indeed, the Founex report outlined many issues which have remained in the debate ever since, including the overriding priority of development for poor countries, the differing environmental priorities of different countries, and the potential international issues raised by domestic environmental policies.

Against this background, the Stockholm Conference brought together representatives of 113 countries and 400 intergovernmental and non-governmental organisations (NGOs), and addressed to some extent the concerns brought forward by both the developed and developing countries. It formally recognised the importance of environmental concerns at the national level and transformed environmental affairs into an international political issue.

---

[4] For a detailed discussion on the preparation and outcome of the Stockholm Conference, see: John McCormick, *The Global Environmental Movement, Reclaiming Paradise*, Belhaven Press, London, 1989.

[5] Miguel Ozorio de Almeida, Wilfred Beckerman, Ignacy Sachs, and Gamani Corea, *Environment and Development*, International Conciliation, Carnegie Document No.586, New York, January 1972.

[6] Richard Sandbrook, 'The UK's overseas environmental policy', in *The Conservation and Development Programme for the UK: A Response to the World Conservation Strategy*, Kogan Page, London, 1983, p.388; cited in McCormick op.cit., p.92.

The agreed documents were the *Stockholm Declaration on Human Environment* and the *Action Plan for the Human Environment.* The Stockholm Declaration, consisting of preamble and 26 principles, addressed the major areas related to environmental issues, ranging from education and science to social and economic development and from resources to pollution.[7] The Action Plan was a functional framework of 109 recommendations and 'consisted of three parts: (i) a global assessment programme...; (ii) environmental management activities; and (iii) supporting measures, such as education and training..'..[8] The interaction of environment and development was formally recognised in the final documents, notably in several principles of the Stockholm Declaration.[9] However, in terms of real commitments in the Action Plan, development issues were not covered in much detail, and only the human settlement policies were addressed in depth.[10]

The Stockholm Conference had several important outcomes.[11] It did a great deal to promote development of national environment policies, notably the creation in many countries of environment agencies and ministries. Extensive national environmental legislation followed, mainly (though not exclusively) in the industrialised countries. At the international level, the United Nations Environment Programme (UNEP) was created as a catalyst for promoting awareness and action concerning environmental issues within the UN system.[12] In addition, the Declaration established a number of principles, such as that of the sovereign right to exploit national resources coupled with responsibility for transboundary pollution, that later became enshrined in international conventions.

---

[7] Edmund Jan Osmanczyk, *The Encyclopedia of the United Nations and International Agreements*, Taylor and Francis, London, 1990, p.874-876.

[8] *Yearbook of the United Nations 1972*, Vol. 26, United Nations Office of Public Information, New York, 1975, pp.318-337.

[9] Principles 8, 11, 13 address this directly; objectives with reference to developing countries also include principles 9, 10, 12, 20, and 23.

[10] *Yearbook of the United Nations 1972*, op.cit., p.322

[11] Maurice Strong, 'From Stockholm to Rio: A Journey down a generation'; in; *In Our Hands, Earth Summit '92*, UNCED Secretariat, Geneva 1991; A. O. Adede, 'International environmental law from Stockholm to Rio, an overview of past lessons and future challenges', *Environmental Policy and Law*, Vol. 22, No. 2, 1992, pp. 88-105, p.88. See also, McCormick, op.cit, p.104-105.

[12] 'Unlike other specialised agencies .. UNEP does not bear the prime responsibility within the UN system for executing projects within its area of concern. Nor does it exist to fund them ... UNEP pursues its goals with a multitude of different partners .. nearly everything UNEP does falls under the headings of catalysis, coordination or stimulation' *UNEP - Two Decades of Achievement and Challenge*, UNEP, 1992, p.8-9.

## 2.3 From Stockholm to the Brundtland Commission

Several initiatives on international environment and development issues followed in the 1970s and 1980s. The Law of the Sea, including measures relating to marine pollution, was negotiated throughout the 1970s and finally completed in 1982. Specific environmental agreements included the London Dumping Convention, the Basel Convention on transboundary movements of wastes, and the Vienna Convention on the Protection of the Ozone Layer (and its Montreal Protocol), together with regional initiatives such as the Mediterranean Action Plan and other regional seas programmes under UNEP, and regional agreements on transboundary air pollution in Europe and North America. A number of North-South agreements were also developed with respect to aid and trade. In addition to these specific agreements, the UN established the Brandt Commission on North-South issues,[13] and the Palme Commission on security and disarmament which also touched upon developmental aspects of militarisation.

Yet concern continued to rise. Environmental problems grew visibly from local to regional and then to the global level. Not only the local impact of specific human activities, but the overall impact of human numbers and behaviour began to receive attention. It became increasingly clear that many of these environmental problems were inextricably linked with broader aspects of social and economic development.

In parallel, efforts on Third World development had to cope with major setbacks. Increasing burdens of international debt, reaching crisis proportions in the early 1980s, undermined the hopes and efforts of many developing countries for secure development; for many in Africa and South America, the 1980s became dubbed 'the lost decade'. There was also increasing criticism of the environmental impact of many of the grand internationally-funded development projects (such as large hydro schemes), and a growing awareness that the pursuit of commodity-export-led growth in developing countries was undermining the environmental and resource base on which they depended.

In 1982, a special session of UNEP's Governing Council was held to review progress since Stockholm, 10 years earlier. The Council concluded that much greater long-term and integrated environmental planning was needed. In 1983, the UN General Assembly called for two major reports to be convened to examine the general issues in environment and development and their interlinkages.

---

[13] *North-South: A Programme for Survival*, Report of the Independent Commission on International Development Issues, Pan Books, London/Sydney, 1980.

The World Commission on Environment and Development, under Norwegian Prime Minister Gro Harlem Brundtland, was established as an independent body 'to re-examine the critical issues of environment and development and to formulate innovative, concrete and realistic proposals to deal with them' and 'to strengthen international cooperation on environment and development ..'..[14] The Brundtland Report analysed the socio-economic and environmental situations of the world and interaction between them.   The overall recommendation was that human activities could and should be redirected towards a pathway of 'sustainable development', with environment seen not as an obstacle to growth but rather as an aspect which needed to be reflected in policies if growth was to be sustained.  Indeed, perhaps the major outcome of the Brundtland report was to crystallise and disseminate this concept.  The phrase 'sustainable development', and its underlying message of the potential for and need to integrate environmental protection with continuing social and economic development, were heavily taken up in public debate and kept in public discussion.

The Brundtland report proposed specific measures for implementation *inter alia*: 'to prepare under UN auspices a universal Declaration on environmental protection and sustainable development and a subsequent Convention', 'to transform this report into a UN Programme on Sustainable Development' and 'an international Conference could be convened to review progress made and promote follow up arrangements ..'..[15]

A parallel report prepared by governments through UNEP's governing council, *Environmental Perspectives to the Year 2000 and Beyond*, provided a framework for national and international action to translate the Brundtland report into practical action. In addition the International Union for the Conservation of Nature (IUCN) published in association with UNEP their broad-ranging *World Conservation Strategy*, which added further impetus to the growing concern and clamour for action. With UN resolution 44/228 in December 1989, the UN General Assembly decided to convene the United Nations Conference on Environment and Development (UNCED).

## 2.4 The UNCED negotiations

This report concerns primarily the agreements developed for and signed at UNCED, which are outlined in the following chapter, and analysed more fully

---

[14]World Commission on Environment and Development (WCED), *Our Common Future*, Oxford University Press, 1987, p.356-357.
[15]WCED, op.cit., p.21, p.23 and p.343.

in Part II. The negotiating context was set by the UN resolution calling for the conference, which stressed the need to reverse environmental degradation, the linkage of environmental and developmental issues, the importance of international cooperation and the developmental priorities of the developing countries. The offer of the Brazilian government to host the conference was accepted and Rio de Janeiro confirmed as its location. The conference date of June 1992 was chosen to coincide with the 20th anniversary of the Stockholm Conference, and UNCED soon became dubbed the 'Earth Summit'.

In parallel with the increasing concern about general issues of environment and development, international concern had been growing (especially in the developed countries) about a number of specific environmental threats. The discovery of the Antarctic 'ozone hole' had made the possibility of human interference with the global environment suddenly seem terribly real, and completion of the Montreal Protocol on Substances that Deplete the Ozone Layer in 1987 raised hopes that other international environmental problems could be addressed through international legal conventions. Mounting concern about human interference with the earth's atmospheric heat balance, and associated predictions of climatic change, led to the establishment first of an intergovernmental scientific panel and then to negotiations on a Framework Convention on Climate Change, with UNCED set as the deadline for the convention to be signed. This background, and the resulting convention, are discussed in Chapter 6 of this report.

Concern about the rapid and accelerating loss of species led to negotiation of a convention aimed at conserving global biodiversity (Chapter 7). In addition, many industrialised countries had hoped that a convention on forests would also be prepared, to form a triad of agreements on the issues of most pressing concern to them, but this proved impossible; as discussed in Chapter 10, it rapidly became apparent that such a convention, primarily involving commitments which involved developing country actions and resources, could not be achieved, and the aim was transformed to a set of 'forest principles' negotiated through the main UNCED process.

Meanwhile, the preparation of UNCED itself proceeded from its launch in December 1989 with an organisational meeting in April 1990 that established two working groups on natural resources and environmental degradation, and a programme involving four formal five-week preparatory committee meetings.[16] The first Preparatory Committee (PrepCom I), Nairobi, August 1990, focused

---

[16]Further details on the PrepComs and negotiations are discussed in, *The Earth Summit Bulletin, A Summary of the Proceedings of the United Nations Conference on Environment*

upon developing the mandate and procedures. It served to define the subjects that governments really wanted to see addressed, and in particular it reflected the concern of many developing countries that their priority of development should not be lost on the environmental agenda. This Prepcom also established the terms for unusually broad participation of NGOs. PrepCom II, Geneva, March 1991, reviewed the detailed background documentation provided by the Secretariat, and established a third Working Group, on institutions and legal issues.

By this stage, it was clear that the negotiations would centre upon two main documents for the conference: a short statement of overall aims and principles, and an 'Action Plan' of specific measures designed to make sustainable development an operational reality. The former, initially dubbed the 'Earth Charter', finally emerged as the *Rio Declaration*, as described in Chapter 8 of this report. The latter expanded into the 40-chapter Agenda 21, summarised in Chapter 9.

The announcement, at this stage, by the UK Prime Minister John Major that he intended to attend the Rio Summit, and the attention devoted to it at the G-7 summit of leading industrialised countries that summer, helped to boost UNCED's growing political profile. PrepCom III met in Geneva in August 1991. The main issue was to decide how to approach the variety of issues for Agenda 21; proposals of the Secretariat on Agenda 21 chapters were discussed and negotiations on the text of the final documents started, but with most of it left open.

The major negotiations on the UNCED texts were thus reserved for the final PrepCom, held in New York in March 1992. During these five weeks, the *Rio Declaration* took its final form, and 85% of the text of Agenda 21 was agreed. The remaining 15%, which contained the more controversial issues, were bracketed and left for final negotiations at the conference in Rio.

## 2.5 The broader process

UNCED was not just a conference, or a series of intergovernmental negotiations. It proved to be a catalyst for a remarkable range of activities. Governments were invited to submit national reports on their environment and development as part of their preparations for UNCED. Although few met the official deadline

*and Development 3-14 June 1992*, Recreio dos Banderantes, 16 June 1992; Koy Thomson, *The Earth Summit Report*, A Report prepared for the Countryside Commission, International Institute for Environment and Development, London, July 1992; Angela Harkavy, *The Earth Summit, The Final Effort*, National Wildlife Federation and CAPE '92, Washington DC, 1992.

of July 1991, by the time of the Summit, reports had been received covering 172 countries and territories - a total which rose to 190 by the end of 1992, with an additional five regional reports. This required effort, study and consultation; many governments established national committees on UNCED issues, with extensive consultation across departments and with NGOs on the UNCED issues. This in turn helped to stimulate interest and supported actions at all levels of society.

There were also many international conferences held around the themes of UNCED, some in support of the official process and some simply riding upon it.[17] Within the UN system, the Food and Agriculture Organisation (FAO) and the UN Industrial Development Organisation (UNIDO) were among those hosting major conferences on how sustainable development might relate to their sectors of activity. The UN also sponsored many other specific conferences which fed into Agenda 21, such as the International Conference on Water and the Environment (Dublin, January 1992).

Governments and UN organisations also collaborated with some of the major NGOs to hold conferences which helped both to spread information and to develop ideas, some of which were later taken up in the official UNCED discussions. Important gatherings were arranged by the International Council of Scientific Unions (Vienna, November 1991) which fed into the associated chapters in Agenda 21 and which helped to map out a programme of global monitoring and research with extensive support from UN bodies and governments;[18] and by the International Union for the Conservation of Nature (the Hague, April 1991). Many other conferences and expert meetings were held on specific areas of the UNCED agenda, for example on Land-based Sources of Marine Pollution (Halifax, May 1991 and Nairobi, December 1991).

---

[17] A survey and analysis of many of these is given in a forthcoming study from the IIASA programme on international environmental negotiations (see Appendix 2). I am grateful to Nitin Desai for emphasising the importance of these parallel processes, and to Pamela Chasek (a contributor to the IIASA studies), and Janos Pastor for background information relating to this section. Further discussion of these parallel processes and NGO inputs is given in, 'Rio: judging its success', *Environment Magazine*, October, 1992.

[18] Results of the conference are published in Jim Dooge et al (eds), *ASCEND '21: An Agenda for Science and Development in the 21st Century*, Cambridge University Press, UK, 1992. This example provides an interesting illustration of the way processes developed around and fed into UNCED. Participants from the ASCEND conference met shortly afterwards with UNCED Secretariat officials to help draft text for the relevant chapters in Agenda 21, partly on the basis of the conference outputs.

Governments also pursued the issues in other fora. Summit meetings of the G7 industrialised countries, the non-aligned movement, the Organisation of positions. Norway, as chair of the Brundtland Commission, hosted (Bergen, May 1991) a Ministerial level conference which sought common ground among OECD countries under the auspices of the UN Economic Commission for Europe. All of the UN Regional Commissions held meetings on UNCED, and some inter-governmental commissions produced reports which developed and defined regional positions on UNCED issues.[19]

Other sectors also sought to organise themselves around UNCED themes. Industries gathered for the 2nd World Industry Conference on Environmental Management (WICEM II), which agreed a Business Charter for Sustainable Development, since supported by many hundreds of companies. A smaller and more focused business group, the Business Council for Sustainable Development, was established with the direct support of the UNCED Secretary General, Maurice Strong. This produced a much more detailed report *Changing Course* for business (see section 4.6 for further discussion of business issues).

UNCED was also a rallying focus for large numbers of disparate environmental and developmental NGOs. Reflecting a great diversity of interests and attitudes, these groups made strenuous attempts to start coordinating their positions and lobbying efforts, primarily around the themes of greater citizens' participation in decisionmaking, a reformed and more equitable international economic order, a more powerful and effective UN, and a far greater degree of environmental protection. NGOs gathered in Paris in December 1991 to work on their own version of an action plan for sustainable development, and to prepare for the NGO Global Forum at Rio. They launched the process of negotiating among themselves many 'alternative treaties', of which nearly 40 were completed in some form, to try and build and communicate a common view of what they would like to see emerge from UNCED (for further details see Appendix 2). The role of NGOs is discussed further in section 4.8.

Indeed a novelty for a UN conference was the greatly strengthened role of NGOs. At formal PrepCom meetings, they were not only observers but they were also allowed to speak and submit written statements. At informal meetings, the NGOs were mainly dependent upon their colleagues who were

---

[19] For example, the Latin American Commission report, *Our Own Agenda*, Inter-American Development/UNDP, 1991, and the report of the Economic Commission for Africa, *African Environment and Development Agenda*, ECA, Cairo, 1991.

members of official delegations. At the final negotiations in Rio, the NGOs were not allowed to participate in the official discussions, but many governments co-opted NGO representatives on to their delegations. With such a level of popular interest, plans were also laid for Rio to be more than just an intergovernmental conference. The UNCED Secretariat encouraged plans for the parallel non-governmental Global Forum, and promoted global media interest. The stage was set for one of the most extraordinary international conference events of the century.

# Chapter 3

## The UNCED Outcome

### 3.1 Introduction

In the first two weeks of June 1992, an estimated 30,000 people converged upon Rio for UNCED. The streets were cleared of the usual city life, the hotels were filled at exorbitant prices. Two independent newspapers dedicated to the conference greeted visitors with the news that the USA had announced its refusal to sign the biodiversity convention, and that the NGOs' Global Forum might collapse after the first week through lack of funds.

For the next two weeks, the media transmitted long-prepared reports on the state of global environment and development, and tried to convey an understanding of the events at Rio - or at least some of them, since there were so many different events in and around the city that it was impossible really to know of all of them, let alone to attend them. Away from the city itself, but very much in the spotlight, the negotiators worked through nights to achieve agreement on the remaining texts which their Ministers could sign. Towards the end of the fortnight, the Heads of State duly arrived to put their signature to the documents, and to deliver short speeches to the two-day Summit at the end of the full conference. Then they were all gone.

What did they sign, and what do the events immediately following UNCED suggest for the significance of this huge event? In Part II of this book, the five individual agreements are explained in some detail. This chapter highlights key features of the agreements, and the immediate follow-up within the UN system which set the official seal upon the recommendations of the Rio conference, and which provides the first insights into how diplomats and governments have reacted to the UNCED process.

### 3.2 The Conventions

Two of the agreements were legally binding conventions, negotiated independently of the main UNCED process, but on schedules set so that they could be signed at Rio.

Negotiations on a treaty to combat 'global warming' were held directly under the auspices of the UN General Assembly, starting officially in February 1991. The resulting *Framework Convention on Climate Change* (chapter 6) provides a legal framework and process intended to address the problem of human interference with the Earth's climate system. The text accepts that climate change is a serious problem, requiring a 'precautionary approach' in the absence of scientific certainty, subject to measures being 'cost effective'. It is accepted that developed countries shall take the lead, and they agree to fund the 'full agreed incremental cost' of measures taken by developing countries, initially through the Global Environmental Facility (GEF). Governments must submit reports to the Conference of Parties on their national policies for addressing climate change, with projections of emissions.

The Convention contains no binding commitments on emissions or levels of international finance, but establishes the decade-stabilisation of carbon dioxide and other greenhouse gas emissions from industrialised countries[1] as an initial 'aim', against which national measures and projections will be assessed. Reflecting dissatisfaction on the part of many countries with the weakness of the commitment, the Conference of Parties is obliged to re-examine the commitments periodically in the light of developing knowledge, and to amend the Convention as appropriate.

At Rio, the Climate Change Convention was signed by 153 governments plus the EC, and others have joined since (see Box 2). The Convention will make it very difficult for governments to evade the issue of climate change, and projections will be assessed against the initial goal of the decade-stabilisation guideline. As of December 1992, many governments were already working on the preparation of national programmes and reports to the Conference of Parties, and most OECD countries had indicated both that they intend to ratify the Convention at the latest by the end of 1993, and that they interpret the emissions guideline as tantamount to an obligation to achieve decade-stabilisation of emissions - a position also adopted by the new US administration after the election.

The **Convention on Biological Diversity** (chapter 7) was negotiated under the auspices of the UN Environment Programme, building on a long history of agreements on specific species and extensive prior discussions on the need for a broader legal basis. The resulting convention seeks to conserve the biological diversity of the planet, through the protection of species and ecosystems, and to establish terms for the associated uses of biological resources and technology. With the majority of threatened biological diversity being in developing countries, and most biotechnology in the North, the central tensions in the

---

[1] The detailed wording is convoluted and deliberately ambiguous (see Chapter 6) but clearly implies that industrialized countries should aim, as a first step, to return emissions of $CO_2$ and other greenhouse gases to 1990 levels by the year 2000, ie. stabilisation of emissions over the decade.

---

### Box 2: Convention Signatories as of December 1992.

The *Framework Convention on Climate Change* was signed by 153 states plus the EC at Rio, and 155 states plus the EC signed the *Convention on Biological Diversity*. Several more states signed later. States that as of December 1992 had only signed one Convention are:

| Biodiversity Convention only | Climate Convention only |
|---|---|
| Kuwait | Argentina |
| Malaysia | Cameroon |
| Panama | Kirbati |
| Qatar | Singapore |
| Turkey | USA |
| United Arab Emirates | Vietnam |

States that as of December 1992 had not signed either Convention are:

| | |
|---|---|
| Albania | Bosnia and Herzogovina* |
| Brunei Darussalam | Cambodia |
| Czechoslovakia | Dominica |
| Equatorial Guinea | Georgia* |
| Grenada | Holy See |
| Iran (Islamic Republic of) | Iraq |
| Kyrgyzstan* | Lao People's Democratic Republic |
| Saint Lucia | Saint Vincent and the Grenadines |
| Saudi Arabia | Sierra Leone |
| Somalia | South Africa |
| Syrian Arab Republic | Tajikistan |
| Tonga* | Turkmenistan |
| Uzbekistan* | |

*States not present at UNCED

---

negotiations were those between the conservation of biodiversity, the control of the benefits derived from exploiting it, and access to biotechnology.

The resulting Convention does not bear the title 'framework' and is more extensive and self-contained than the Climate Change Convention, whilst similarly lacking specific commitments. It affirms that States have the 'sovereign right to exploit their own resources', whilst ensuring that such activities 'do not cause damage to the environment of other States' or other areas. States shall aim to share 'in a fair and equitable way the results of R&D and the benefits arising from commercial or other utilisation ..'. on 'mutually agreed terms'. This shall include access to technology 'on fair and most favourable terms', whilst being 'consistent with the adequate and effective protection of intellectual property rights'. Developed countries shall meet the 'agreed full incremental costs' of developing country measures under the Convention. Parties are to develop 'national strategies, plans or programmes' for protecting biodiversity, and communicate information on them to the Conference of Parties, though the requirements in this area are weaker and less specific than in the Climate Change Convention.

A number of developed country governments are uneasy about the powers given to the Conference of Parties in regard to funding requirements, and entered reservations to that effect. The USA refused to sign the Convention because of fears about the perceived threats to its biotechnology industry from safety and patenting requirements, and concerns about the financial arrangements. Others signed, but many entered statements clarifying their understanding of the financial arrangements. The Convention requires ratification by just 30 countries to enter into force, but ratification by some developed countries (including the UK) is likely to depend upon these clarifications concerning the financial implications.

## 3.3 Non-treaty agreements

In addition to the two Conventions, three non-legally-binding agreements were signed at Rio by nearly all the participating countries.

**The Rio Declaration on Environment and Development** (Chapter 8) presents 27 principles of environment and development, intended to 'build upon' the Stockholm Declaration of 1972: 'in order to achieve sustainable development, environmental protection shall form an integral part of the development process' (Principle 4). Many of the principles address development concerns; they state a 'right to development' and highlight the special needs and circumstances of the developing countries, especially the poorest, and stress the need for development and poverty alleviation, and access to financial and technological resources. Principles concerning trade and environment are ambiguous and to an extent inconsistent; others concern the role of special groups. As compared to the Stockholm Declaration, 'the problems of the *Rio Declaration* are more to do with implementation, blame and responsibility' (p.89).

**Agenda 21** (reviewed in Chapter 9) is intended as the action plan for achieving sustainable development. It consists of 40 chapters covering 500 pages, which address (i) general issues of social and economic development; (ii) issues of specific national and other resources; (iii) the role of different major groups; and (iv) means of implementation. It is not a binding treaty, but it carries far more political authority than a report from an expert group or commission: it is 'perhaps best seen as a collection of agreed negotiated wisdom as to the nature of the problems, relevant principles, and a sketch of the desirable and feasible paths towards solutions, taking into account national and other interests. Thus it stands as a grand testimony and guide to collected national insights and interests pertaining to sustainable development' (p.90). As such, it will form a basic reference document of 'good practice' for many years to come.

Many themes recur throughout Agenda 21. These include a 'bottom-up' approach of putting emphasis upon people, communities and NGOs; the need for 'open governance'; the importance of adequate information; the need for adequate cross-cutting institutions; and the complementarity between regulatory approaches and market mechanisms for addressing development and environmental needs. In general, Agenda 21 really does seek to integrate environment and development, and succeeds in highlighting the linkages between many different specific issues. It incorporates some performance goals, though many of these are reaffirmations of ones previously agreed. Crude estimates by the Secretariat of the financial requirements for implementing Agenda 21 led to the figure of $125bn/yr international finance, which roughly equates to the UN goal for Overseas Development Assistance (ODA) of 0.7% of GNP from industrialised countries. In the event, little if any additional money was forthcoming for its implementation (see Appendix 1).

Agenda 21 calls for a 'Commission on Sustainable Development' as the major follow-up institution within the UN system, recommending this to be a forum of high level representatives, reporting to the UN Economic and Social Council, empowered to oversee the implementation of Agenda 21 including financial issues. More specific results of Agenda 21 include recommendations to start negotiations on a desertification convention, and to hold conferences on the sustainable development of small island states, and on the management of straddling and migratory fish stocks.

The final agreement at UNCED was a statement on *Principles of Forest Management* (Chapter 10), which took the place of a putative forest convention. Echoing other UNCED documents, this emphasised that governments have the sovereign right to exploit the forests within their national boundaries, but also the responsibility to ensure that their activities do not negatively affect other countries. It notes various other general principles, but no more specific commitments; it is a 'document with something for everyone, without any clear message or direction'.

## 3.4 The UN aftermath

As a UN Conference, UNCED reported ultimately to the political authority of the UN General Assembly. The specific elements of the agreements negotiated through UNCED (as opposed to the Conventions) consisted of recommendations for action to be taken by the UN General Assembly. Considering and acting upon the output from UNCED formed one of the main tasks of the subsequent 47th Session of the UN General Assembly which concluded in December 1992.[2]

To those concerned that the output from UNCED would be further weakened by UN politics at the General Assembly, the decisions were reassuring. The UN General Assembly passed seven resolutions relating to UNCED. The first, 'enabling resolution', strongly endorsed the outcome of Rio and urged governments and all relevant bodies to ensure full and effective implementation of the UNCED agreements. Review of the implementation of UNCED agreements is to become a standing item in subsequent annual UN General Assembly sessions, with a special session devoted to a review of progress in 1997.

The other resolutions followed through the specific recommendations in Agenda 21. The longest and most important, on 'Institutional Arrangements to Follow Up the UNCED' (see Box 3), endorsed the recommendations of Agenda 21, Chapter 38 and directed the Economic and Social Council 'to set up a high-level *Commission on Sustainable Development* .. in order to ensure the effective follow-up of the Conference.' .. The General Assembly resolution restated and emphasised all of the roles for the CSD set in Agenda 21, its central theme being '.. to examine the progress of the implementation of Agenda 21 at the national, regional and international levels.. in order to achieve sustainable development in all countries'.

---

[2] This report was held back so as to be able to incorporate results of the UN General Assembly deliberations, and went to press shortly afterwards.

The CSD will consist of representatives from 53 states on three-year terms, 'at a high level, including ministerial participation'. The CSD is also to provide for other governments, UN bodies and non-governmental groups 'to participate effectively in its work and contribute within their areas of competence to its deliberations'. The full Commission is to meet once a year for a period of 2-3 weeks, and will adopt a multi-year thematic programme of work targeted towards a complete review by 1997.

Several complementary structures were also established. A *High-Level Advisory Board* is established to report directly to the UN Secretary General. This 'should consist of eminent persons broadly representative of all regions of the world, with recognized expertise ... drawn from relevant scientific disciplines, industry, finance and other non-governmental constituencies ..'.. An *Inter-Agency Committee* is also established. To support all this, the General Assembly called for a 'highly qualified and competent secretariat support structure' to be established 'as a clearly identifiable entity' (ie. a permanent body with a significant degree of independence).

The other General Assembly resolutions enacted the other specific institutional recommendations of Agenda 21, namely:

- Negotiations to develop a Convention to Combat Desertification are to start with an organisational session in February 1993, with a view to finalising the convention in 1994.
- A global Conference on the Sustainable Development of Small Island States will take place in 1994 in Barbados. It will have the twin aims of developing plans for their development including sustainable utilisa tion of their marine and coastal resources, and of adopting measures that will enable them to cope effectively with externally induced environ mental changes (primarily, potential sea level and storm intensity changes).
- A global Conference on Straddling and Highly Migratory Fish Stocks will be established in 1993 with the task of formulating recommenda tions 'with a view to promoting effective implementation of the provisions of the UN Convention on the Law of the Sea'.
- An official 'World Day of Water' is established annually on 22 March, which shall be a focus for promoting the recommendations in Chapter 18 of Agenda 21.

**Box 3: Extracts from the UN General Assembly resolution establishing the Commission on Sustainable Development**

The General Assembly,

Welcoming the adoption by the United Nations Conference on Environment and Development of Agenda 21 ...

1. Endorses the recommendations on international institutional arrangements to follow-up UNCED as contained in Chapter 38 of Agenda 21, particularly on the establishment of the high-level Commission on Sustainable Development;

2. Requests the Economic and Social Council .. to set up a high-level Commission on Sustainable Development as a functional commission in accordance with Article 68 of the Charter of the United Nations in order to ensure the effective follow-up of the Conference .. fully guided by the principles of the Rio Declaration on Environment and Development and all other aspects of UNCED, in order to achieve sustainable development in all countries;

3. Recommends that the Commission shall have the following functions as agreed in paragraphs 38.13, 33.13 and 33.21 of Agenda 21:

A. To monitor progress in the implementation of Agenda 21 and activities related to the integration of environmental and developmental goals throughout the UN system through analysis and evaluation of reports from all relevant organs, organizations, programmes and institutions of the UN ..

B. To consider information provided by Governments, including, for example, in the form of periodic communications or national reports regarding the activities they undertake to implement Agenda 21 ..

C. To review the progress in the implementation of the commitments contained in Agenda 21, including those related to provision of financial resources and transfer of technology;

D. To review and monitor regularly progress towards the United Nations target of 0.7% of GNP for ODA...

E. To review on a regular basis the adequacy of funding and

Box 3 continued . .

mechanisms, including efforts to reach agreed objectives of Chapter 33 of Agenda 21..

F. To receive and analyse relevant input from competent non-governmental organizations, including the scientific and the private sector, in the context of the overall implementation of Agenda 21;

G. To enhance the dialogue within the framework of the United Nations with non-governmental organizations and the independent sector ..

H. To consider, where appropriate, information regarding the progress made in the implementation of environmental conventions which could be made available by the relevant Conferences of Parties;

I. To provide appropriate recommendations to the General Assembly.

J. To consider .... results of the survey to be conducted expeditiously by the UN Secretary-General of all UNCED recommendations for capacity-building programmes, information networks, task forces and other mechanisms ...

6. Recommends that the Commission will consist of representatives of 53 States elected by ECOSOC ... at the high level, including ministerial participation...

7. Recommends further that the Commission should:

(a) provide for representatives of various parts of the United Nations system and other inter-governmental organizations .. to assist and advise the Commission in the performance of its functions ...and participate actively in its deliberations;

(b) provide for non-governmental organizations, including those related to major groups as well as industry and the scientific and business communities, to participate effectively in its work ..

12. Recommends that the Commission should adopt at its first substantive session a multi-year thematic programme of its work .. that would integrate in an effective manner related sectoral and cross-sectoral components of Agenda 21 in such a way as to allow the Commission to review the progress of the implementation of the entire Agenda 21 by 1997.

The final General Assembly resolution gives official blessing to the 'Capacity 21' initiative of the UN Development Programme, for following through the capacity building proposals in Chapter 37 of Agenda 21.

The General Assembly thus endorsed and implemented the specific recommendations of UNCED, without significant backtracking and indeed without undue acrimonious debate. The permanent home of the CSD has become a politicised issue which is unlikely to be resolved before its first organisational meeting in New York. Many of the developing country concerns about financing and technology transfer were repeated and reflected in what is now standard language, and all (including the developed countries) lamented the paucity of financial commitments. The overall impression however is that, far from being an attempt to downgrade or weaken the issue of sustainable development as some had feared, the negotiators sought to ensure that the integration of environmental issues with enhanced development efforts will form a central part of the UN's agenda over the forthcoming years.

In other spheres too the immediate follow-up to UNCED gave a similar impression. By Christmas 1992, UNEP had established in its Geneva offices the Secretariat for overseeing the Biodiversity Convention. The Negotiating Committee of the Climate Change Convention reconvened in December to develop its work plan for preparing for the first meeting of the first Conference of the Parties, with the realisation that many specific issues need to be addressed rapidly. The GEF met in Abidjan in December 1992, and made a start on the process of restructuring its governing structure (see section 4.7), apparently with success adequate to ensure its future role as the central multilateral funding agency for global environmental concerns, and to enable the next round of donations to proceed. In the non-governmental sector, the UNCED Secretary-General Maurice Strong established an 'Earth Council' of independent specialists to provide independent input, and to strengthen the political voice of existing highly respected groups such the International Council of Scientific Unions.

The six months following Rio thus confirm that UNCED was about much more than education, public relations and media hype; the immediate follow-up has established international institutional mechanisms which are intended to start implementing sustainable development. To understand some of the problems which these processes will face, the issues which may arise and the extent to which progress may be made, requires first and foremost an understanding of the themes emerging from UNCED itself.

Chapter 4

Themes and Lessons

UNCED was the largest international conference ever held. It was, furthermore, not merely an immense event, but the culmination of a preparatory process - indeed, a series of parallel preparatory processes - spanning nearly five years since the initial international discussions which followed publication of the report from the World Commission on Environment and Development, with more than two years of formal negotiations. Many general observations can be drawn from this and the resulting conventions and other agreements.

## 4.1 A process towards a process ....

The UNCED agreements contain few clear commitments addressed to specific environmental and developmental needs. Many held hopes for binding undertakings on a range of issues, from targets for limiting greenhouse gas emissions and for forest preservation, to creation of lists of threatened species or areas rich in biodiversity for special protection, together with agreed funding levels for the implementation of the conventions and of the many issues mapped out in Agenda 21. Such hopes were dashed. The lack of clear commitments led many to brand UNCED as a failure, yet others considered the fact of agreement itself, on such an immensely complex agenda, a remarkable achievement.

Certainly, things could have been worse: had other governments followed the USA in its refusal to sign the Biodiversity Convention, or had the USA backed Israel in its attempt to remove references to the 'rights of peoples under occupation' in the *Rio Declaration*, developing countries might well have retaliated with other refusals or objections, and the whole process could have started to unravel. Most governments were relieved just to have got to the 'finishing' line of having agreements signed. UNCED did result in an unprecedented global dialogue on the issues, and as observed by the Executive Director of the UN Environment Programme, Mostafa Tolba, experience in international environmental affairs teaches that 'we must walk before we can run, and crawl before we can walk'.[1] As sketched in the next chapter, UNCED has established new potential and new avenues for the pursuit of sustainable development.

In the UNCED agreements, the substitute for specific commitments are thus ones of process, sometimes backed up by non-binding goals. The follow-up

---

[1] Mostafa K. Tolba, Address to the Plenary at UNCED, Rio, 4 June 1992.

to the Climate Convention includes assessment of progress in relation to the guideline emission stabilisation and mandatory re-examination of the existing 'Commitments' section. Agenda 21 establishes Commission on Sustainable Development to oversee the implementation of Agenda 21, with reaffirmation of the UN goal for ODA funding from rich countries of 0.7% of GNP accepted by most countries (not the USA), though with a timetable accepted only by a few. Agenda 21 also points towards a number of other processes under way within the UN system, such as the 1994 UN Conference on Population and Development, which might further its many causes.

Furthermore, as outlined in the previous chapters, UNCED engendered many other developments within and outside governments. Many of these persist, not only in terms of the knowledge gained and perceptions changed, but also in the form of new institutional developments and networks for promoting goals of sustainable development.

Nevertheless, as the culmination of such an extensive process itself, building on the 20 years since the Stockholm Conference and the five years since the Brundtland Commission, the lack of clear policy commitments must be recognised as troubling. The agreements are hardly convincing demonstrations that countries are yet ready to tackle seriously the major changes required to bring sustainable development much closer to reality.

Arguably, UNCED was unlucky. It occurred at a time of global recession, and with the GATT negotiations in an unsettling state of suspended animation. The US Bush Administration was one which had consistently displayed little sympathy for developmental or international environmental issues, and at the time was obsessed primarily with domestic economic issues in the run-up to the 1992 Presidential Election. The EC, which had been squaring up to fill the leadership vacuum left by the US position, ran into complex internal difficulties over the process of EC integration and consequent harmonisation of environmental and development policies. Japan, perhaps the only country which seemed set to offer large increases in international assistance, was (and is) still finding its place in the world, nervous of straying too far from the US fold or of being seen as a general international monetary source. The government was also beset by domestic difficulties, and in the event Prime Minister Miyazawa was unable to attend Rio.[2]

---

[2] This was due to a critical emergency debate in the Japanese Diet. A video film of the Prime Minister's speech, potentially one of the most significant contributions to the Summit, could not be shown at the plenary because of fears that this would set a dangerous precedent.

Yet any event must face its difficulties, and other aspects were favourable. The disintegration of the Soviet empire removed the crushing divide which had undermined most global endeavours of the previous decades, and could have been used to free the immense resources which had been locked into that confrontation. Also, UNCED was launched on an unprecedented wave of popular concern.

Some substitution of process for commitments is an inevitable fact of international negotiations, particularly on such vast and complex issues such as those raised by UNCED, but the attention given to follow-up processes varied greatly between the different negotiations. For the Climate Convention, there had been discussions since the opening of negotiations on national strategies[3] and 'pledge and review' processes (a concept which was dropped in name, but partly re-emerged in substance);[4] its follow-up may prove to be relatively effective (see the following chapter), though this is far from assured. The Biodiversity negotiations involved far less emphasis on follow-up, although the Nairobi meeting which concluded the Convention also drew up proposals for future action which has to be endorsed by UNEP's 1993 Governing Council. Efforts on forests were focused mostly on (failed) attempts to open negotiations on a convention. For Agenda 21, fundamental decisions about the nature of the follow-up process only began to be seriously debated in UNCED in the last few months before the Summit.

Commitments cannot always be eschewed in favour of new processes; the evasion of key measures has to stop, and the procreation of new processes cannot continue indefinitely. Yet surveying the vast expanse of Agenda 21, it was always obvious that any binding commitments at UNCED would be small in relationship to the problems overall, and that is likely to remain true for each individual step taken in the future. What is required are processes which (foster the political conditions required to) spawn a steady accretion of effective and meaningful commitments. The next chapter discusses how far the explicit follow-up to UNCED may meet this requirement.

---

[3] W.A.Nitze, *The Greenhouse Effect: Formulating a Convention*, RIIA, London, 1990; A.Chayes, E.B.Skolnikoff, D.Victor, *A Prompt Start: Implementing the Framework Convention on Climate Change*, Report from the Bellagio Conference on Institutional Aspects of International Cooperation on Climate Change, January 1992, Harvard Law School/MIT Centre for International Studies.
[4] *Pledge and Review: Proceedings of a Workshop convened by the Royal Institute of International Affairs*, RIIA, London, 1991.

## 4.2 The North-South divide: economics and finance

The central issue with which all future attempts to promote globally sustainable development will have to grapple is that which formed the most pervasive feature of UNCED, namely the division between rich and poor, developed and developing, North and South. The differences receive emphasis in almost every section and every Article of every document associated with UNCED.

Most developing countries approached UNCED with a mix of fear and hope. The fear was that environmental issues would intrude in the form of new constraints on their development, and new conditions on aid received from rich countries: the intrusion of Northern concerns on the Southern priorities of development and poverty alleviation. The hope was that these Northern concerns about the potential environmental implications of Southern development at last gave the South some real leverage in global politics: if the North wanted them to change their future behaviour and development paths, they would have to meet Southern demands. The scale of hope was clearly expressed by the South Centre:[5]

'Two strategic considerations should guide the South's negotiating position... (a) ensuring that the South has adequate 'environmental space' for its future development, and (b) restructuring global economic relations in such a way that the South obtains the required resources, technology, and access to markets ...

In the UNCED negotiations proper, the South should ... insist on tilting the balance towards development and considerations of global economic reform, in order that the South may be offered some hope of being able to follow a path of sustainable development. Issues on which the South should receive firm commitments from the North are: (i) debt relief; (ii) increased ODA, (iii) .. access to international liquidity; (iv) stabilisation and raising of commodity prices; and (v) access to markets in the North'.

In the end, hardly anything became of such hopes. The fundamental determinants of international economic relations remain precisely the same - if anything, the developing world would get more from a successful GATT round which opens Northern markets to their commodities, than they have got from UNCED. The interminable references to the special circumstances of developing countries are nothing to do with restructuring international economic

---

[5] *Environment and Development: Towards a Common Strategy of the South in the UNCED Negotiations and Beyond*, South Centre, Geneva/Dar-es-Salaam, November 1991.

relationships, and little to do with enhanced aid; they are simply protective clauses which assert that developing countries are not committed to anything unless additional money is made available. Since it is clear that money is not remotely available on a scale which is comparable to the estimated needs (see Appendix 1), this can be seen as casting an immense shadow over the whole UNCED exercise.

In other respects, too, the outcome reflected the balance of economic power and interests to a far greater degree than developing countries had hoped. Thus, the global issues which were of greatest concern to the North received a high profile relative to issues such as water quality, which are far more pressing in terms of the quality of life and indeed survival in developing countries. The Conventions clearly reflect this. Agenda 21 did something to redress the balance, but in the end it seems unlikely that the 'Southern' issues will receive as much attention as those of the North, nor perhaps as much financial support, though these featured highly in the estimates of financial requirements (see Appendix 1).

From a moral perspective, it is easy to place the blame for the inadequacy of resources and other commitments, and consequently of likely implementation, squarely on the fact that the rich countries were prepared to offer so little. In the context of the climate negotiations, a leading negotiator wrote that:[6]

'It is difficult for most of the developing countries to accept the proposition that they should enter into commitments which would adversely bind them, either now or later on, for the sake of a problem caused by the developed countries - who neither wish to equitably share the remaining emission reserves in the atmosphere, nor to share (even in a small way) the benefits and resources that they have built up by plundering the world's greenhouse gas reservoir capacity'.

In terms of *realpolitik*, additional factors undermined the prospects for solutions emerging.[7] First, many developing countries over-rated the bargaining

---

[6] Tariq Osman Hyder, 'Climate negotiations: the North/South perspective', in I. Mintzer (ed), *Confronting Climate Change: Risks, Implications & Responses*, CUP, Cambridge, UK, 1992.
[7] The following comments refer primarily to the attitudes suggested by negotiating stances adopted throughout most of the negotiating process. Some individual analysts may well have perceived the problems in advance, and the head of the Pakistani delegation to both the Climate Negotiations and the talks on restructuring the GEF wrote an eloquent assessment of developing country perceptions and prospects in the months running up to UNCED (Hyder, ibid). Such insights were too few and too late to have much impact on the negotiations.

power which environmental issues gave them. Developed countries were concerned, but there was little indication that they were ever frightened enough to be subject to crude 'greenmail', as some called it (ie. implicit threats about the global environmental consequences of unconstrained development, used as a lever to extract more financial and technological transfers). A confrontational approach was never likely to work in the developing countries' favour. A more cooperative approach at the outset, on a common basis which more fully reflected the negotiated phrase of 'common but differentiated responsibilities' might have got further, but from an early stage, negotiations were grounded in the history of North-South conflicts dating back to the 1970s debates of the 'New International Economic Order' and before.

Second, the demands of developing countries on some important issues seemed unclear in detail. General remarks about the need to restructure international economic relationships had little impact without closer specification. If commodity prices should be higher than the natural market rate, who should support them and how? What kinds of debt were to be written off, and what kinds of mechanisms or guarantees might reinstate the confidence required to enable any further loans, if those were sought? A number of detailed proposals have been presented in the course of general international economic debates, but having accepted the basis of international market principles, the proposals at UNCED were often unclear, and in practice such discussions often boiled down to the question of financial and technology transfers: developing countries were caught in a vicious poverty trap, and as such they deserved transfers which might help them get out of it, and demanded them if they were expected to take on any new obligations or costs. Finance, as always, proved the vital, inevitable, but perhaps ultimately destructive rallying point for disparate Southern interests.[8]

---

[8] 'The UNCED agenda, as it was defined in the preparatory process, set the stage for a remarkable come-back [by the G-77 developing country group]. Once the issue of money is brought to the forefront, all LDC governments can rally behind a common demand for concessions from the West. This glosses over the internal differences among them and creates a united, external front. No other issue has had such a galvanising effect on the third world in the forty-year history of north-south bargaining, and such a destructive impact on international collaboration .. very little has changed in the argument on both sides since the 1960s ...' (Helge Ole Bergesen, 'Empty symbols or a process that can't be reversed? A tentative evaluation of the institutions emerging from UNCED', *International Challenges*, Vol.12 No.3, 1992).

The developed countries for their part were prepared to agree to language on preferential and concessional access to technology, as long as these terms were undefined and thus did not undermine the concern above all of the USA to protect the basic principle of patent rights as the reward for private enterprise. Also, after considerable pressure from the rest of the OECD, the USA was persuaded to agree to widespread references concerning the need for 'new and additional resources'[9] for developing countries, as long as specific numbers were not entailed.

Third, developing countries did not adequately appreciate the nature of the political constraints faced by developed countries (the reverse of course is equally true, and should be borne in mind throughout this discussion), and the political requirements which might make large-scale transfers or other changes possible. It may or may not have been apparent that raising taxes to give money to poorer countries was not a vote winner in most developed countries, and especially in the more insular USA. It was, however, always obvious that the donor countries would not agree to large-scale transfers unless they had faith that the money would be well used, and not wasted or dissipated, for example through corruption. That clearly meant both that conditions would be attached to transfers, and that they would have to be managed by an institution in which the donor countries had some faith.

The former - 'green conditionality' - became a very emotive topic, but there was never any real alternative if large transfers were to be countenanced under the UNCED umbrella. The latter factor meant that agreement on the institutions for controlling transfers had to be reached before substantive discussions about the scale of transfers could be opened. In the event, developing countries had to accept a compromise in the form of a reformed and democratised Global Environment Facility with the World Bank as a lead agency (see discussion on Institutions below), but this was only achieved in the month before UNCED itself (with important details still to be resolved), which was far too late to open substantive discussions on quantities and applications of aid.

---

[9] As with many international texts, the language here is critical. In debates surrounding the Montreal Protocol, the USA agreed to language on 'new' resources, but later indicated that it considered that these might be diverted from other international assistance; hence the term 'new and additional'.

As developing countries complained, this remains an unsatisfactory situation in part because the GEF is intended only for projects with global environmental benefits. Developing country requests for a separate 'Green Fund' for implementing the multitude of non-global issues considered in Agenda 21 met with the response that since the whole point of the exercise was to integrate environment in development, a separate fund was not appropriate. Yet no alternative was suggested by the developed countries, other than references to a possible 'Earth Increment' attached to the next round of International Development Assistance loans - a hope which few developing countries found convincing, and which indeed rapidly disappeared in the cold financial light of actual recession-induced development aid (see Appendix 1).

One lesson from all this is that expectations and debate focused far too much on the scale of resource transfers, and not enough on their quality, applications, and control - the issues which were bound ultimately to determine the scale of resources made available.


## 4.3 The North-South divide: population and consumption

Economic issues were not the only axis of North-South confrontation. Another important dispute lay along the dimension of debates about population, poverty and consumption levels. This was most explicit in negotiations over Agenda 21, although elements of the debate emerged in negotiations over all the UNCED agreements.

Clearly, population is a critical element in sustainable development. More people, at a given level of *per capita* consumption, means more pressure on land, food, energy and a wide variety of other environmental resources. Of pressing concern, rapid population growth can also undermine attempts to raise living standards especially where there is high unemployment: population growth outstripped economic growth in much of Africa during the 1980s, and more pessimistic projections suggest that *per capita* income in Africa may continue to decline.

Twenty years ago, most developing countries reacted strongly against international attempts to discuss population targets and control. Understandably it is a delicate personal issue for many people, of a kind in which attempts at control by the state can raise powerful emotions, and demands by one country upon another are bound to be extremely contentious. Yet population issues clearly have a logical place at the heart of any discussion on long-run sustainability.

In the event, the UNCED negotiations indicated that many developing countries recognised the importance of population issues and the validity in principle of discussing them. Many after all already have population policies in place (some have been of such an intrusive nature that governments have been forced to retreat), and regularly press for more assistance to enable them to pursue feasible population policies. Despite this, population proved a contentious and highly politicised issue.

This was partly because of the inherent political difficulties raised by any international attempt to interfere on such an emotive topic. But more pointedly, developing countries noted that environmental impact is the *product* of population and consumption levels, and at present most of the global environmental problem is caused by the 20% of the global population in the rich countries. Consequently, developing countries linked the population debate in Agenda 21 directly with the chapter on consumption patterns. At one time in the PrepComs, indeed, the relevant chapters were negotiated side-by-side, with trade-offs being made between different paragraphs in each. Since there was little political will to discuss consumption levels (see also below), this resulted in tenuous negotiations which weakened language on aims related to population.

Northern governments, for their part, came during the negotiations to recognise the uselessness and inadvisability of pursuing yet more calls for population control targets that could not be implemented. What matters is the reproductive choice of people, not declarations of government-inspired population targets. Thus the Agenda 21 chapter on population came to reflect an approach, based not upon largely irrelevant population control targets but upon the issues of family security, knowledge, child mortality, women's rights and access to 'reproductive health techniques' which could actually affect the reproductive behaviour of people. The language on family planning and contraception in Agenda 21 is, however, weak (the terms themselves are never mentioned), not primarily because of North-South conflict, but because of Catholic-inspired opposition notably from the Holy See and from the Philippines.

Consumption levels, a counterpoint to population levels in the environmental dialogue, formed a final issue underlying the complex North-South brew. As negotiations proceeded, developing countries made frequent reference to the fact that the industrialised countries were the major consumers and polluters, and should take clear action to address their own profligate levels of consumption before trying to tell developing countries to act differently: 'physician, heal thyself'.[10] As noted, in the Agenda 21 negotiations language on population was directly tied to the extent to which developed countries were prepared to accept references to the problems posed by 'excessive consumption' and the need to curtail it. Also, developing countries feared that Northern consumption levels would deprive them of 'environmental space' in which to develop, and some saw high levels of consumption, as opposed to investment, as part of the global problem of capital scarcity.

And yet, the details of 'Northern sustainability' were never seen as an important part of the UNCED agenda in their own right. In part, developed countries felt they were already initiating efforts, and had indeed made considerable progress in cleaning up various kinds of pollutants especially over the past few years, and thus did not need this subject to international scrutiny. Yet there was a fundamental paradox in the fact that UNCED participants almost universally interpreted the 'D' (development) to mean the process of poor countries getting richer, along an economic path similar to that followed by the industrialised countries, whilst the whole point of the 'E' (environment) was to encourage such countries to 'leapfrog' that path of development to a wealthy but sustainable state. If the end-point is supposed to be so radically different from the current resource-intensive pattern of industrialised countries, a central question has to be how the already industrialised countries are supposed to develop towards such a state. Sporadic attacks by some developing countries on the consumption patterns of the North, and the need to encourage cleaner technologies, did not amount to any clear vision of alternative paths for *Northern* development - such questions were simply not addressed in detail. There seemed little recognition of the fact that the UNCED agenda was incoherent unless 'development' was broadened to include questions about the future development of industrialised countries. This was not only because the industrialised countries were keen to avoid such politically awkward discussions, though that was clearly an important factor. For many developing countries also such issues may have seemed a diversion from their development agenda. Indeed, if the developed countries did start to address such issues about their own future development more seriously, it could have considerably strengthened their moral position and thus increased pressures on the developing countries

[10] Some kinds of environmental stress decline with increasing wealth, but despite the popular adage in UNCED that 'poverty pollutes', most pollutant emissions and resource pressures are greater from the richer countries (World Bank, *World Development Report 1992: Environment and Development*, World Bank, Washington, 1992; J. Parikh, *Consumption Patterns: the Driving Force of Environmental Stress*, Indira Gandhi Institute of Development Research report to UNCED, Bombay, 1991).

to accept more responsibility towards altered development goals. Only in the closing stages of negotiations did it seem that some NGOs began to argue the fundamental importance of addressing questions of Northern development within UNCED.

The overall result of these diverse factors is that all the UNCED texts seem far removed from the ideal of a global partnership. Indeed, the unending references to the special situation and needs of developing countries seems more akin to a global apartheid in which countries are forever divided into 'developed' and 'developing'. This was not imposed, or opposed, by any group; it was quickly established as a consensus approach from which there was hardly any dissent, because it was clear that rich and poor could not be treated alike. Yet it seems a poor basis on which to build a 'global partnership for sustainable development' in the 21st century.

## 4.4 National interests and the diversity of nations

This should not be taken as indicating that the Northern and Southern groups were reasonably homogenous. Indeed, the international community is far more heterogeneous on environment and development than yet acknowledged. Within the OECD, there were clear divisions of attitude between the USA, the EC and Japan not just on the climate issue and on the signing of the Biodiversity Convention, but also on far broader questions of approaches to developing country concerns. Canada, Australia, and New Zealand, as well as the Nordic countries tended to form different groups again, generally more sympathetic to developing country concerns. The transition economies formed another distinct group, far apart from the OECD on many economic questions.

The developing countries form an even more diverse group. This is partly because of their very different sizes and levels of economic development - India, for example, has an industrial economy comparable in size with the UK, and the quality of its research institutes, etc., match many smaller OECD countries (thought the extent to which the fruits of this were evident in negotiations was, as with many other countries, questionable). 'Developing countries' also encompass such rich countries as the Arab oil states.

Yet beyond such economic differences, on many environmental issues the interests of developing countries diverge fundamentally. The prime environmental concern of most African countries is with desertification and other land degradation, with climate change potentially a powerful if apparently distant threat that could amplify their suffering. Concerns about the impact of global warming on sea levels are greater for the small island states, and countries such as Bangladesh and Egypt which depend heavily on very low-lying coastal regions. Such countries lobbied for a precautionary approach, and lamented the weakness of the Climate Convention. They achieved a specific programme area on small island states in Agenda 21, and commitments to hold an intergovernmental conference on their development.

Yet to the oil-exporting countries, the threat is precisely the opposite - that people will start to do something about climate change. In the end, Saudi Arabia and Kuwait didn't sign the Climate Convention, and placed reservations on the atmosphere chapter of Agenda 21. Many of the large and rapidly industrialising developing countries were also notably distant in attitudes from the smaller, weaker and perhaps more vulnerable developing countries that often seemed keener to reach effective agreements. With such divergences, it seems doubtful how relevant the G77 can be as a group in future negotiations on such issues: claims upon funding form almost the only common denominator. Indeed, divisions along entirely different political lines, perhaps even cutting across the North-South divide, can be envisaged.[11]

On forests and biodiversity also there were potent differences. Many of those with large untapped forests saw forest policy as an issue of national sovereignty and resisted attempts by the international community to consider forests as an issue of legitimate international concern and attention. Other developing countries recognised also the international and global concerns associated with deforestation, and indeed some (such as Bangladesh) considered that they suffered directly from their neighbour's deforestation.

Thus the negotiations revealed major divisions within the different economic groups, a feature which deepened the more specific the negotiations became. This should have been no surprise: UNCED was a testimony to the fact that national interests operate in environmental politics much as in other areas, and that these interests differ in complex ways between nations.

## 4.5 Sovereignty and governance

Sovereignty is a word often used in international negotiations. Obviously, it is a concept of key importance, preventing one state trying to force its own cultural, political and policy preferences upon other which may have perfectly

[11] M.Paterson and M.Grubb, 'The International politics of climate change', *International Affairs*, Vol.68, No.2, pp293-310, April 1992.

valid reasons for differing values, priorities, mechanisms and capabilities. Yet during UNCED, at times it seemed to become almost a totem with which many developing countries sought to ward off discussion on various uncomfortable issues, as well as a means of defence against potentially onerous or inappropriate environmental demands of the North. As such it became a symbolic word, treated as an absolute, and used as a way of trying to block a number of areas of discussion, most notably on forests.

However, for all its genuine importance promoted further by rhetoric, sovereignty in reality is not absolute in the international arena any more than it is in the EC or other less integrated regional groupings. It is a complex, many-faceted and relative concept which may be amended in pursuit of national and mutual benefits. The UK Prime Minister of more than 30 years ago acknowledged that 'Practically every nation, including our own, has already been forced by the pressures of the modern world to abandon large areas of sovereignty and to realise that we are now all interdependent'.[12] In the UNCED debates and their follow-up, it is not hard to see echoes of the emotive debates and posturing in Europe which eventually gave way to the acceptance that 'Sovereignty is not like virginity, which you either have or you don't ... it is a resource to be used, rather than a constraint that inhibits or limits our capacity for action'.[13]

Some greater flexibility with respect to sovereignty appears a necessity if the political dialogue on global sustainability is to advance much further. The opening of negotiations on a desertification convention may bring this factor closer to recognition, as noted in the next chapter. There is, however, a serious practical issue which this raises concerning the strength of governmental institutions, or weakness thereof - the classical distinction between 'hard' and 'soft', or 'strong' and 'weak' states.[14]

Amongst the developing countries, those with strong governmental authority were in a position to propose and negotiate alternate forms of agreement, sometimes strong ones, and to call for strong international authorities to oversee them. At UNCED, the Malaysian foreign minister stated that 'problems of environment and development exist at national, regional and

---

[12] H. MacMillan, *Britain, the Commonwealth and Europe*, Conservative Political Centre, London, UK, 1962, p.7.

[13] Sir Geoffrey Howe, 'Sovereignty and independence: Britain's place in the world', *International Affairs*, Vol. 66, No. 4, pp.675-695, October 1990.

[14] Gunnar Myrdal, 'The Soft State', *The Challenge of World Poverty*, Allen Lane, London, 1970, Penguin, 1971, Chapter 7.

international levels. Therefore the resolution of these issues requires action at these three levels', and he reiterated Malaysian proposals for a binding and monitored global forestry agreement which would commit all countries to maintain 30% forest cover or fund forests elsewhere to compensate for a failure to achieve this aim.[15]

However, a number of developing countries especially are 'soft' states, in which governments do not have the administrative control with which to implement such a commitment. For example, the Amazon is such a vast and remote area that it may be extremely difficult for the Brazilian government to control some of the activities which cause deforestation - a situation reinforced by the fact that many powerful interests, both industrial and military, perceive clearing the forest to be an essential part of Brazilian development. In cases where governments are unable to control such forces, they can hardly enter into specific binding agreements concerning them; insistence on absolute sovereignty, such as that displayed by the Brazilian government, is a natural defence against such difficulties.[16]

In general, such limitations at home makes it difficult for the governments concerned to enter into meaningful commitments to the international community, and the political embarrassment of being forced to reveal such weakness creates a powerful incentive to use sovereignty as an absolute defence against intrusion of the international community into a country's domestic affairs, however appealing in theory the mutual interest may be.

---

[15] Statement by the Honourable Dato Abdullah Haji Ahmad Badawi to UNCED, Rio, 10 June 1992; *An Initiative for the Greening of the World*, Ministry of Science Technology and Environment, Malaysia, April 1992. The Malaysian proposals served to emphasise that their government's intense opposition to forest agreements of the form proposed by developed countries was not based upon an approach of absolute sovereignty, but in large part upon differing perceptions of equity. Given the fact that countries differ greatly in their current and historic forest cover, land resources and population densities, this was not a very practical proposal. Nevertheless, the willingness to talk in terms of targets, mechanisms and monitoring requirements contrasted sharply with other countries' refusal to countenance any such intrusion on their sovereignty. The fact that this proposal could in principle form an opening gambit for negotiations on a binding agreement, combined with the Malaysian advocacy of the need for strong international supervision of global environmental problems, emphasise the point.

[16] Raphael Kaplinsky, "The international context for industrialisation in the coming decade," *Third World Industrialisation in the 1980s: open economies in a closing world*, Special Issue *Journal of Development Studies*, Vol.21, No.1, 1984, pp75-96.

To some extent, related obstacles face many large and diverse democracies, such as India and indeed the USA. In such political systems, enacting policies which cut across the interests of powerful groups or regions can be politically very difficult. In such cases, even if the Head of State signs an international agreement it may not guarantee implementation. There is no easy solution to this conundrum, but it is a factor which, in its varied forms, may have an important bearing upon what is possible in international negotiations.

## 4.6 Regulatory policy, business, and the environment

The surge in environmental concerns of the late 1980s led to renewed environmental pressures on business, and pressures upon governments to implement environmental policies that would directly affect business. This in turn led the business community itself to take a greater interest in environmental issues, and to become engaged in the UNCED process. In some cases this took the form of traditional lobbying efforts - the US coal industry, for example, usually had an active presence at the Climate negotiations (and discussions of the Intergovernmental Panel on Climate Change (IPCC)), and tried hard to influence the US position against any wording which could increase the pressure for action to limit $CO_2$ emissions.

Others however recognised that business needed to be seen to be taking a more positive approach, and there were a number of initiatives. The International Chamber of Commerce (ICC), representing several hundred major companies, produced a *Business Charter for Sustainable Development*,[17] a set of voluntary guidelines for good business conduct. The Business Council for Sustainable Development, a smaller and more focused group set up by senior managers of major companies with the encouragement and support of the UNCED Secretary-General Maurice Strong, produced a report *Changing Course*.[18] This took a broader view; it emphasised business responsibilities, but also said clearly that governments had the responsibility to set appropriate regulatory frameworks. *Changing Course* also emphasised a view that environmentally-friendly companies would in the long run be the successful ones, a marked contrast to statements from other parts of the business community (and their sympathetic governments) which presented environment as a threat to business. The theme

---

[17] International Chamber of Commerce, *The Business Charter for Sustainable Development: Principles for Environmental Management*, ICC, Paris, 1991 (leaflet).
[18] S.Schmidheiny et al, *Changing Course: A Global Business Perspective on Development and the Environment*, MIT, Cambridge, MA, USA.

that environmental leadership would be profitable was not limited to the Business Council, nor was it just words; some major companies had by the time of Rio made considerable efforts at environmental clean-up well beyond regulatory requirements.[19]

The UN Centre on Transnational Corporations (UNCTC) was also requested by the UN to prepare a submission to UNCED for Agenda 21. The UNCTC has for many years coordinated discussions on the development of global guidelines for the regulation of transnational corporations (TNCs), and negotiations under UNCTC auspices on 'codes of conduct' have been under way (shortly before the UNCED meeting, the Centre was merged and renamed in a general re-organisation of the socio-economic UN organisation, but much of its work continues). The UNCTC Secretary-General's report to UNCED[20] drew upon this experience and suggested a number of actions, including proposals for greater accountability, a 10-year goal for harmonising company-level environmental accounting and reporting procedures, and environmental pricing.

In the event, the activities of business received a low profile throughout UNCED. A chapter in Agenda 21 emphasises in rather general ways the need for good business conduct, and there are some other more specific references (eg. with respect to waste management and toxic chemicals). In general, however, the impact on business is only implicit in the altered parameters of sustainable development. The approach is thus more akin to that of the Business Council or the ICC, than that suggested by the UNCTC ; with the exception of calls for 'environmental pricing' (which came from many quarters), their recommendations were not significantly taken up except in the most vague terms.

This outcome reflected several disparate themes. To some extent it reflected the non-interventionist approach of much of the discussions, and the consequent focus upon broader government policy in setting the environmental and hence market context. Also, doubtless some governments were reluctant to engage

---

[19] As well as being an attempt to reinforce a "green" image, such companies emphasised the value in improving energy and other resource efficiency, reducing the risk of environmental liability, and establishing a leadership position for a more environmentally conscious world (see *Changing Course*, op.cit, and P. Schwartz et al "Modifying the mandate of existing institutions: corporations" in I. Mintzer (ed), Confronting *Climate Change: Risks Implications and Responses*, CUP, Cambridge, UK, 1992).

[20] UN Centre on Transnational Corporations, *Transnational Corporations and Sustainable Development: Recommendations of the Executive Director*, Report of the Secretary-General, ECOSOC E/C.10/1992.2, 16 December 1991.

such powerful interests, given that the biggest multinationals earn more than the GNP of most of the countries participating at UNCED. In addition however, the activities of the Business Council and other industrial efforts raised hopes that a considerable degree of self-regulation was feasible for moving industry beyond minimum standards set, if any, and this reduced pressure for an official 'code of conduct' (the UNCED Secretary-General Maurice Strong, who helped to initiate the Business Council, clearly supported this approach).

On broader issues of regulatory policy towards the environment which affect business behaviour, the UNCED texts reveal clear trends in the debate towards consideration of market-based principles and policies. The agreements contain references to economic instruments, encouraging governments to examine and consider their use, and call (in qualified ways) for 'environmental pricing' - pricing which reflects environmental impacts and resource depletion. This was not presented as a panacea which provides an 'alternative' to other measures, but rather as a potentially important component of policies within a regulatory framework set by governments. The need for freer international trade was also reiterated, with expression of concern that environmental measures should not impede trade.

These discussions did reveal clear limits in the debate on environmental policy, in the form of conflicts or contradictions which were never seriously discussed or faced. Some of the most environmentally conscious companies have started to stress that there are limits to how far 'self regulation' can proceed before it starts to affect companies' competitive position; and that in this respect it is unreasonable to expect companies to do more unless their competitors are required to do so as well. This sounds like a call for governments to set clear environmental standards; and, in the context of traded goods in a freer international market, to do so internationally. There is a clear tension between an approach which eschews such international oversight in favour of voluntary and unilateral measures, whilst simultaneously calling for a more harmonised trade regime.[21]

Furthermore, the calls for environmental pricing, whilst clear, are set in a very abstract way. The blunt fact is that environmental pricing means that the

---

[21] This is a politically complex issue which again involves North-South concerns. Developing countries and their industries, starting from a lower base of environmental protection and more dependent upon resource-intensive industries, fear the impact of being forced by international standards to adopt the same level of environmental protection and costs as developed countries. See the discussion of Rio trade principles in Chapter 8.

prices of environmentally damaging goods and processes are raised above their natural market prices, which means that someone collects the additional economic rent. Questions of whom, and how, were not addressed explicitly, although obvious answers include respectively governments, and environmental taxes. The clarification and implementation of the words at Rio thus face serious conflicts, as illustrated by the fierce industrial opposition to proposals for implementing environmental pricing in the form of carbon or other taxation.

## 4.7 International institutions

Almost all international institutions are potentially affected by the implications of 'sustainable development' and the UNCED agenda. Many existing institutions receive mention in the UNCED agreements, especially Agenda 21. Not surprisingly, the main focus is upon the institutions broadly of the UN family, including the Bretton Woods multilateral financial institutions of the World Bank, the IMF, and GATT.[22]

The World Bank emerged somewhat enhanced by the outcome of the debates on mechanisms for funding. As noted above, developing countries and many NGOs had pressed for a separate 'green fund' to implement Agenda 21, but the donor countries were not persuaded of any logical need for such a separate fund for general environmental aid when a major point of the exercise was to try and integrate environment and development concerns. In the end, existing institutions including the pilot GEF, led by the World Bank in conjunction with the UN Environment Programme (UNEP) and the UN Development Programme (UNDP), was the only mechanism available in which they had sufficient confidence. Before the Summit, agreement was reached in principle on the need to restructure its governance to make it more democratic, accountable and transparent.[23] On this basis, the GEF now has negotiated status as the interim funding mechanism for the Conventions, and for the relevant 'global environmental issues' in Agenda 21. Details still remain to be resolved and uncertainties persist about its exact role and the degree of funding commitments (see Appendix 1).

---

[22] Discussions during the UNCED process established that these bodies, whilst not "UN bodies", were to be regarded as part of the broader "UN system".

[23] *Statement on the Future Evolution of the Global Environmental Facility*, Report of meeting, World Bank, 29-30 April, 1992 . Thirty-two governments, half from developing countries, agreed a final document (*The GEF - Beyond the Pilot Phase*) which set revised guiding principles for the GEF.

The most concrete institutional achievement of UNCED was the creation of the high-level *Commission on Sustainable Development*, as described in the previous chapter. Even before its formal creation, some hailed the CSD as the saviour of UNCED.[24] Others are much more pessimistic, suggesting that it will become another highly politicised and unproductive forum for sterile debates.[25] Even after the General Assembly resolution, its real impact is difficult to assess,[26] though the high level annual meetings may provide a focal point for political efforts and media interest in the issues.

With the exception of the CSD and its affiliated bodies, UNCED illustrated continuing reluctance by governments to consider new institutions. Early in the UNCED process for example, many non-governmental groups with the backing of some governments proposed the need for an international agency to promote energy efficiency and renewable energy sources, as a balancing complement to the existing International Atomic Energy Agency, which to date is the only UN body directly concerned with energy matters. The proposal was advanced in draft texts of Agenda 21 but fiercely opposed by the oil producing countries, and the proposal was removed as it became clear that many other governments were reluctant to consider such additional institutions.[27]

The outcome for existing UN institutions is also difficult to assess. UNEP and UNDP receive consistent mention, in addition to their role as coordinators of the GEF. UNEP is expected to continue its 'catalytic role' among the UN agencies, extending international co-ordination of scientific and political work. UNDP, in addition to its existing field work activities, is expected to

---

[24] Hilary French, 'Hidden success at Rio', *WorldWatch*, Vol.5, No.5, Washington, September/ October 1992, p.7-8.

[25] 'The Commission on Sustainable Development is unlikely to increase accountability. Like its sister commission for human rights, it will probably emerge as a highly politicised forum where governments will exchange views and accusations, and where states will align and realign to defend their interests and perceived by the people in power at any particular time' (Helge Ole Bergesen, 'Empty symbols or a process that can't be reversed?', *International Challenges*, Vol.12, no.3, 1992).

[26] Peter Thatcher, 'Evaluating the 1992 Earth Summit - an institutional perspective', *Security Dialogue*, Vol. 23, No,3, pp117-126, 1992, offers a more complex but still hopeful view of the CSD's role.

[27] An outline of proposals was presented in 'Solar energy solutions for an environmentally sustainable world: recommendations to UNCED', International Solar Energy Society, Boulder, CO, USA, 1991. The outline was elaborated and pursued by an *ad hoc* UN committee which fed it into the Agenda 21 process.

play 'the lead role' in capacity-building, eg. in helping to develop national 'sustainability plans' and in establishing the institutional framework required to further goals of sustainable development within countries. Shortly after UNCED, UNDP started to pursue this responsibility with an outline 'Capacity 21' initiative.

There are, however, many different ways of interpreting the institutional thrust of Agenda 21, especially when set against actual deployment of resources (or lack of them). The International Institute for Environment and Development describe the outcome for existing UN bodies as 'equivocal', namely:

> Chapter 38 [of Agenda 21] stresses that UNDP has 'a crucial role' in the follow-up to UNCED but it avoids the key issue of how UNDP's mandate relative to the rest of the UN system could be strengthened and how it could be provide with additional resources. UNEP should equally be 'enhanced and strengthened' and is envisaged to undertake new roles, for example provide technical and policy advice to governments on the integration of environmental aspects into development programmes. There is recognition that the agency would require additional resources to do this, but there is no commitment by governments to provide them. UNCTAD receives such a tepid mention that it must be questions whether it now has any role at all, as most initiatives on trade are taken in the context of GATT.
>
> There is talk in chapter 38 about the need for regional and sub-regional cooperation, but there is surprisingly little emphasis on the regional development banks, the only regional institutions with significant resources. The sectoral chapters of Agenda 21 dutifully make mention of the UN specialised agencies concerned. However, the profile of the UN agencies overall in the UNCED documentation is low, even when it might have been expected not to be ... there is little in the UNCED documentation to contradict the thesis that UN system reform is long overdue.[28]

This may be too pessimistic. The value of UNEP's role is clearly recognised and enhanced, and capacity-building is a crucial activity for which UNDP has clear lead authority. Also, UNCTAD was given new life at its Council meeting in Cartagena in March 1992, and redirected as a body with a mandate for greater research, and less negotiation, including explicit reference to trade and

---

[28] 'International institutions', in *12 lessons from UNCED, Perspectives*, Special Issue, p.46, International Institute for Environment and Development, London, 1992.

environmental issues. More generally, UNCED has clearly strengthened the role of the UN overall. The principle has been accepted that the UN must oversee the development of a body of international agreements and processes on the environment, ensuring universal participation in the negotiations.

Clearly, however, there is no dramatic change at the international level, any more than at the national level, of the kind that many consider necessary if global development really is to become 'sustainable'. The question is more whether the formal strengthening will be matched with adequate resources and political authority given by member countries to the new and strengthened bodies. Bergeson concludes his pessimistic review by recalling the words of the Brundtland Commission which helped to launch the whole process:

> The Commission gave a prediction, which is worth repeating five years, and a long process, later: 'We are aware that such a re-orientation on a continuing basis is simply beyond the reach of present decisionmaking structures and institutional arrangements, both national and international'. UNCED is another confirmation that they were right, which points to an intriguing institutional 'Catch 22': you cannot change the institutional structure without changing the institutional structure.[29]

Bergesen admits his conclusion to be tentative; the next few years will help to show whether the assessment is right.[30]

---

[29] Bergesen, 'Empty symbols or a process that can't be reversed?', op.cit. ref[25].

[30]Shortly before going to press, a major article on the institutional implications of UNCED was published, which echoed several themes in this study and explored the role of UNEP in particular in much greater depth. It concluded: 'Governments expect "the UN" to "coordinate" policies for "sustainable development" that governments themselves do not pursue . . . . UNEP as a node of good science, funded to the tune of [a good university], could genuinely catalyse the international community. This is something that UNEP can do. But "coordinate" a system that was 25 years old before it was created, it cannot do, and should no longer be asked to do. The creation of the CSD recognises this.... Does the Commission have any better prospects of achieving the twin objectives, that integration shall triumph over sectoralism and the coordination shall vanquish duplication? . . . . this is the second chance to update the machinery. It is also a second opportunity to embark upon a round of bureaucratic inflation. However, it is from the imaginative easing of the debt burden that the greater resources for basic needs and infrastructure investments will arise inside the Third World, and with that, the capacity of these countries to collaborate with the North in the implementation of international agreements.' (Mark Imber, 'Too many cooks? The post-Rio reform of the United Nations', *International Affairs*, Vol.69, No.1, 1993, pp55-70).

## 4.8 The role of non-governmental groups

UNCED was unique not only in its size. Throughout the preparatory process, it also had greater participation from NGOs[31] than any previous major international conference, as outlined in Chapter 2. Popular pressure had been instrumental in creating the concern that led to UNCED, and on many specifics, non-governmental groups were recognised to be better informed than many of the governments involved. The UNCED Secretary-General Maurice Strong emphasised from the first day the positive contribution that such groups could make to the process, and sought to give them unprecedented (though still limited) access to the PrepComs; at the first PrepCom, vocal support from the USA, the UK and some other developed countries helped to overcome resistance from some other governments to allowing such participation. Many governments, especially but not exclusively those from the industrialised countries, co-opted non-governmental personnel on to their delegations at Rio.

There is little doubt that NGOs made major contributions to the process, and that their status concerning such issues has in general been raised. Obviously, one cannot generalise too far, both because viewpoints differ and because NGOs themselves span an enormous range. Nevertheless, despite the persistent criticisms they levied at governments and their negotiators, it seems that most of the officials involved felt that NGO contributions were on balance positive, and sometimes critical.

The NGOs themselves tasted greater access and influence in international politics, and will not easily be wholly excluded from future events, even if governments wanted to do so, which seems doubtful.[32] The UNCED agreements in general lay significant emphasis upon the need for transparency and publication of material, which automatically gives NGOs greater access. Agenda 21 in particular encourages their involvement more explicitly, at a range of levels. The UN Secretary-General will be advised by a high-level advisory board of independent experts (A21:38.18). Additional developments, for example the establishment by Maurice Strong of the 'Earth Council' to

---

[31] The term NGO literally applies to all non-governmental actors, including research establishments and industrial lobby groups. It is, however, most frequently used in the context of groups which lobby for greater action on environment or development issues, and is used here with this meaning unless otherwise specified, though some comments apply to all forms of non-government groups.

[32] For a detailed discussion see N. Dubash et al "Modifying the mandate of existing institutions: NGOs" in I. Mintzer (ed), *Confronting Climate Change: Risks,Implications and Responses*, CUP, Cambridge, UK, 1992.

provide independent appraisal of sustainable development issues and strengthen the voice of expert groups, reinforce this impression. Several new networks of independent advisors to senior officials within governments and the UN are likely to be established. The UK government, following a pledge made by Prime Minister John Major at Rio, hosts in 1993 a major international conference to explore more fully the role that NGOs can play.

All this fits in well with trends in the social science literature on regime theories, which increasingly see non-governmental processes as far more important in shaping policy and societal changes than is generally given credit; such literature also stresses their growing international importance.[33]

Yet despite all this enthusiasm, there are clear limits. In some countries, NGOs are now expected - especially by environment ministries and sympathetic ministers - to help in all kinds of ways, from helping to implement 'grass roots' changes such as small-scale recycling schemes, to involvement in education, and even in policy analysis and preparation, for example with politically practical proposals on how to operationalise some of the recommendations in Agenda 21. Above all, embattled government departments now look to NGOs to generate sufficient public support to enable them to get their policies through reluctant government machinery. Increasingly this could include requests from sections of government to generate popular support for such politically difficult measures as eco-taxes and higher taxes for overseas aid. It seems possible that in the quest for sustainable development, far from NGOs being ignored, they may be asked to shoulder more of the burden of practical policy development. This of course is far more difficult than simply raising concern and criticising governments, and it is unclear how much they can really deliver.[34]

---

[33] S.Andersen and W.Ostreng (eds), *International Resource Management*, Belhaven Press, London / Fridtjof Nansen Institute, Oslo, 1989; Oran R. Young, *International Cooperation: Building Regimes for Natural Resources and the Environment*, Cornell University Press, Ithaca, NY, USA, 1989.

[34] One researcher from a development charity in the UK expressed to the author a fear that, far from having too little credibility, NGOs now had too much. The fear expressed was that NGOs were being asked to solve problems that required governmental resources and were rightly the province of governmental leadership - an ironic echo of the complaint by the UN Secretary-General Boutros Ghali that the UN itself is suffering from too much credibility, and is being asked by governments to solve complex conflicts for which it had nether the political authority nor the resources (B.Boutrous Ghali, speaking at open General Meeting at the Royal Institute of International Affairs, London, 3 July 1992).

Another issue is that, as NGOs gain more influence, not only their limitations but also the differences between them become sharper. Divergences between environmental and developmental NGOs were apparent from an early stage in the UNCED process, and substantial efforts were made to narrow the differences. Yet, at UNCED, the gulf between the biggest US environmental NGOs and many Southern NGOs in particular seemed almost as huge as that between their respective governments on some (though not all) issues. Frustrated by the slow progress and lack of commitments in the official process, NGOs negotiated 'alternative treaties' (see Section 2.6). These negotiations between the NGOs at UNCED were certainly not as difficult as the official negotiations, but they were hardly easy, and it requires little imagination to foresee the depth of disputes had they been negotiating real policy and trying to take account of the full range of viewpoints and affected parties (for example by including NGOs from industry or trade unions). This may be of little surprise to students of political science, but was to say the least disconcerting especially for the more idealistic NGOs attending UNCED.

## 4.9 The politics of publicity and pressure

A related feature of UNCED is that the event clearly was not only aimed at governments and their agreements. Maurice Strong always envisaged it as the greatest show on earth, a global media event which would force the issue of environment and development on to every TV screen. Aided enthusiastically by NGOs and the media itself, without doubt he succeeded. He hoped that such coverage would generate political pressures that would force substantive agreements. Certainly, political pressure was generated - newspapers around the world bemoaned the weakness of the agreements and lambasted their politicians for selling out the future of the planet - but powerful agreements to change policies did not materialise.

The approach had clear benefits in terms of popular education, though it also inevitably risked reaction against such extensive coverage - the journalist who wrote that after a week at UNCED, all he wanted to do was 'to go out and kill a few trees'[35] cannot have been alone. It also helped to get Prime Ministers and Presidents to Rio, which provided a deadline, focal point and opportunity for signing the various agreements under the eyes of the world. These were not

---

[35] Chris Cragg, *Energy Economist*, August 1992.

inconsiderable benefits. But whether or not all the hype really helped to get better agreements seems more questionable. The overall result was a pale shadow of what Maurice Strong and others had hoped for, and at UNCED the divisions between countries seemed as deep as ever.

The outcome to some degree reflects the style in which Maurice Strong led the conference. He gave great emphasis both to high politics and popular involvement. His exertions helped to raise the profile of UNCED and the issues involved, to get Heads of State to Rio, and to disseminate the message worldwide. There were also endless meetings of negotiators to try and find political compromises when conflicts arose. Yet less effort was devoted to studies to clarify the practical implications of sustainable development and the areas of inherent tension arising from fundamentally differing interests, or to consultations which might have increased understanding of different positions and explored ways of accommodating them, and thus built more consensus on the practical measures to be taken. Despite the vast financial sums being discussed for example, there were few early initiatives for specialists to explore the central issue of control of resource transfers, and no open review of how costs were estimated; the Secretariat's costs estimates for Agenda 21 were finally largely ignored by the negotiators and politicians, if not by the NGOs and media (see Appendix 1). One of the few extended efforts within the UN system to build consensus among warring factions of economic analysts over potential costs for example was launched away from UNCED, at the personal initiative of UNEP's Executive Director.[36] The degree of strategic thinking about the follow-up to UNCED was also unclear, until the closing months before the Summit when it became impossible to ignore the fact that the real test of UNCED would lie almost entirely in the aftermath.

In short, UNCED demonstrates that trying to bludgeon governments into agreements with exhortation, moral pressure and threats of environmental doom is not enough. To get effective agreements, governments need to

---

[36] 'Report on consultative meetings on the costs of limiting greenhouse gas emissions held in London and Washington, 1991', UNEP, Nairobi, 1992, *UNEP Greenhouse Gas Abatement Costing Studies*, UNEP Collaborating Centre, Risø National Laboratory, Denmark. The IPCC itself, established jointly between UNEP and WMO in 1988, did a great deal to build consensus understanding of the nature of the climate problem. It was prevented from examining economic issues before UNCED by a number of developing countries, who feared that this would be highly politicised and driven by Western economic ideology.

understand the issues, the implications of responses, and the political perceptions and forces involved. Excessive and over-simplified publicity can indeed make consensus-building more difficult especially if it points in different ways in different countries, as occurred to some extent over North-South issues at UNCED. Generalised publicity and popular pressure are important in generating generalised political will; but they are not enough.

Chapter 5

The Road from Rio

## 5.1 Introduction

Writing shortly after the close of UNCED, the Deputy Secretary-General of the Conference, Nitin Desai, suggested that UNCED had had four major achievements:

> First, it has secured a set of agreements between Governments which mark significant advance in international cooperation on development and environment issues. Second, it has secured political commitment to these agreements at the highest level and placed the issue of sustainable development at the heart of the international diplomatic agenda. Third, it has opened new pathways for communication and cooperation between official and non-official organisations working towards developmental and environmental ends. Fourth, it has led to an enormous increase in public awareness of the issues that were tackled in the process.

> All of these elements are interlinked - the action programmes, the political commitment, the open and transparent processes, and the public awareness reinforce each other. Together, they constitute a significant first step in the transition to sustainable development.[1]

These are not inconsiderable achievements, but the emphasis is upon the final sentence: UNCED was a 'first step'. This echoes a theme in almost all comments by the time of the Rio conference: despite the lengthy build-up and preparatory process, UNCED was the beginning of a process. With UNCED over, what then can be said about the specific nature of this follow-up process?

## 5.2 Convention processes

The detailed discussions in Chapter 6 and 7, on the two Conventions signed at Rio, illustrate the importance of the follow-up processes. The clearest path has been set by the Climate Change Convention. This has sought to compensate for the uneasy and ambiguous compromises concerning emission commitment by

[1] Nitin Desai, 'The outcome of Rio', *Network '92*, No.18, Centre for Our Common Future, Geneva, June/July 1992.

establishing an unusually emphatic follow-up process. The negotiating committee will continue meeting to prepare for the first meeting of the Conference of Parties, which must be held within a year of the Convention entering into force, which given the current pace of ratification will probably mean in late 1994. The Conference of Parties will meet annually thereafter; it is required to examine the existing commitments in the light of accumulating scientific evidence; and it is empowered and encouraged to amend the Convention should the commitments and programmes be deemed inadequate.

To support this, Signatories are required to submit their 'national strategies' detailing measures being undertaken, which will be subject to some form of (as yet unspecified) scrutiny by the process. The IPCC will also continue meeting; at its plenary in November 1992 it agreed a structure of new assessments, including economic studies which had previously been considered too controversial, for the period up until the first Conference of Parties.

Those deeply concerned about the outcome may ask, if countries would not agree on limiting emissions or other substantive measures in 1992 despite the evidence available, then why might they a few years later? It is a valid question, but it is also evident that better understanding of the nature of the problem, and of the options for limiting emissions, still needs to penetrate through political systems before significant steps are politically feasible. The Climate Convention certainly does not ensure that adequate action will be taken, but that is in the nature of the uncertainties and political forces involved; the process established goes a long way towards encouraging the requisite political conditions. A drawback indeed may not be an inadequacy of follow-up meetings, but an excess, if there are so many meetings that those involved never have the time to read, learn, and think about the issues involved - a frequent complaint in the hectic two years running up to UNCED.

The follow-up to the Biodiversity Convention is less emphatic. The bodies established are similar, and the Conference of Parties will similarly meet within a year of the Convention entering into force with a mandate to 'keep under review the implementation of this convention'. As with the Climate Convention, entry into force may be unusually rapid, but as noted in Chapter 3 key developed countries may not ratify for some time at least. Also as compared with the Climate Convention, the Conference of Parties is not specifically required to 'periodically examine the obligations of the Parties and the institutional arrangements .. in the light of the objective'. The Biodiversity Convention thus appears to focus more upon the substance agreed, with less emphasis upon the formal follow-up.

Concerning forests, key developing countries did not only fight off pressures for a Convention in the run-up to UNCED, they also successfully resisted pressures at UNCED for any clear commitment to start such negotiations; there are implications that a convention may only be considered once the Forest Principles have been 'implemented', whatever that means.[2]   The Indian magazine[3] *Down to Earth* concluded enthusiastically that 'Developing countries came out of UNCED with the firm conviction that they had gained considerable time in their struggle against a forest convention.  As Malaysian ambassador Ting Wen Lian put it, "We have not even given them a window. We have just given them a chink"'.

It is hard to see how progress on the forests issue can be made when key developing countries appear to regard any attempt to discuss the possibility of a forest convention as fundamentally against their interests, and so many participants appear to lack confidence in the existing agencies such as the UN's Food and Agriculture Organisation. Given that some of the developing country resistance stemmed from their resentment at the way forests were sometimes discussed in terms of 'carbon sinks' for emissions from developed countries, progress may become more feasible if and as developed countries adopt constraints on their greenhouse gas emissions. There are, however, still central issues of perceived national interest and sovereign control over natural resources at issue.  The outlook for a coordinated international effort to limit deforestation, then, seems particularly bleak, though agreements with particular developing countries are more feasible. Given the central role of forest habitats in maintaining biodiversity, and of their significant role in the global balance of greenhouse gases, this failure may have far broader repercussions.

Largely separate from any of these three issues was the clear undertaking reached at Rio to launch negotiations for a convention on desertification (Agenda 21, Chapter 11), subsequently enacted by the General Assembly. This was largely at the insistence of the African countries, to whom desertification is by far the most important environmental threat, and who complained bitterly

---

[2] 'These principles reflect a first global consensus on forests. In committing themselves to the prompt implementation of these principles, countries also decide to keep them under assessment for their adequacy with regard to further international cooperation on forest issues' (Forest Principles, Preamble); Agenda 21 states as an objective '.. on the basis of the implementation of these [forest principles] to consider the need for and the feasibility of all kinds of appropriate internationally agreed arrangements to promote international cooperation on forest management' (Agenda 21, 11.13(e)).

[3] Anil Agarwal and Sunita Narain, 'Forests of Global Contention', *Down to Earth*, Delhi, 15 July 1992.

about the low profile given to desertification on the UNCED agenda. The Convention will address the environmental degradation that has the greatest impact on people in some of the poorest countries in the world, and as such represents an important feather in the UNCED cap.

However, it is striking that desertification is a local and regional phenomena, certainly in impacts and also to a large extent in cause (though climate change may come to be an important factor). It remains unclear, therefore, quite how and why this will be addressed in an international convention, and the agreement to launch these negotiations has two interesting implications. First, it is an indication that there may be a role for international conventions in addressing essentially local issues. Second, part of the resulting deal will inevitably involve agreement on the actions to be taken within affected countries to stem desertification, in return for international assistance - a clear example of sovereignty as a 'resource to be used, rather than a constraint' (p.35) which cuts directly across the absolutist argument wielded by 'forest countries' against the prospect of a forest convention.

Thus, although explicit attempts to link negotiations on desertification with those on deforestation were defeated at Rio, the agreement to proceed with negotiations on the former undermines the two central arguments used to resist a forest convention, namely those of locality and absolute sovereignty. Given the hardened positions on a forest convention, it may take a long time to translate this into practical results; but the 'chink' to such an agreement can only widen.


## 5.3 The broader agenda

The overall follow-up to the grand design of Agenda 21 is also difficult to assess. As outlined in section 3.4, the follow-up debates in the UN established the CSD and supporting structures, and launched the UNDP's Capacity 21 programme. These, combined with the general (but probably inadequately funded) recommendations concerning the strengthening of UNEP and UNDP, suggest that UNCED has succeeded in leaving an indelible mark upon the UN system, with an institutional process of review and pressure which is not going to disappear.

There are also many specific issues for which some form of follow-up is already planned. In addition to the opening of negotiations on a desertification convention, these include major UN conferences, for example those on the development of Small Island States, the management of Migratory Fish

Stocks, and the 1994 Conference on Population and Development. More generally, all the ideas surrounding the concept of capacity-building for achieving sustainable development exist in Agenda 21, together with innumerable more specific suggestions concerning policies towards resources and pollution management, special groups, etc.

Nevertheless, of the thousands of 'thou shouldst' commandments in Agenda 21, most are generalisations which are hard to define or measure, and hardly any of them are backed up by adequate resources (see Appendix 1), certainly not in terms of international financial commitments, but also often not in terms of domestic resources even in the industrialised countries. Chapter 8 of Agenda 21 states that 'Governments .. should adopt a national strategy for sustainable development based on, *inter alia*, ... Agenda 21' (8.7(d)). There are many indications of what might constitute such strategies, but few are in a form that can be clearly verified against objective criteria.

There is no explicit requirement for governments to report on such strategies or more generally on their implementation of Agenda 21, but this is recognised as desirable and most countries are expected to do so. However, the scope, depth and structure of reports is not well specified, and nor does Agenda 21 specify a process of review. The CSD will presumably try to develop clear guidelines and procedures, but trying to coordinate and interpret potentially over 100 widely varied national reports on such an immense agenda is bound to be a messy, difficult and contentious process.

The lack of additional financial resources is a major constraint, with both psychological and substantive impacts. Psychological, because it raises questions (especially to developing countries) about how serious developed countries are about the UNCED agenda. Substantive, because many aspects of Agenda 21 will not happen without additional resources, or will only happen very slowly, simply because developing countries have other financial and political priorities. It is, however, wrong to suppose, as many have claimed, that Agenda 21 is meaningless without additional finance. Many other aspects of Agenda 21 are to do with policy and process changes that depend less upon additional finance than upon political imagination and commitment.

Financial constraints will highlight a generic though probably unavoidable limitation to Agenda 21, in that it sets no priorities. Everything is seen as important, serious, urgent. Agenda 21 gives little clue as to whether, with limited resources, efforts should for example concentrate upon population measures, human settlements, or poverty alleviation; energy, forests or water. In practice, defining such priorities internationally may be almost impossible (in part because priorities will differ between countries); but lacking the human and financial resources to implement everything, choices will have to be made.

The result of all these factors is to place immense weight on the new institutions, particularly the CSD (which is also invited 'to consider, where appropriate, information regarding the progress made in the implementation of environmental conventions' (A21:38.13(f)). As noted in the previous chapter, there are many different views concerning the CSD. Some lauded it as the saviour of Agenda 21 before it was even formally created, whilst others are much more cautious. It is charged with overseeing the implementation of a massive and often vague agenda when the processes which might deliver the tools required (such as national reporting) have not been clearly established; the resources pledged for implementing Agenda 21 are negligible; and the resources and powers accorded to the CSD itself may yet prove to be rather constrained. Even if the elements of Agenda 21 had been more clearly defined and measurable, it could not force governments to enact the commitments if they did not wish to do so.

It would, however, be a great mistake to see the follow-up to Agenda 21 issues solely in terms of whether there is clear path mapped out, with an international policeman to monitor it and financial agreements to fund it. For that is not the nature of the document, nor of the issues. At the international level, other follow-ups will be important in addition to the institutional changes established by UNCED and discussed in the previous chapter.

For example, a strong consensus was built during the Agenda 21 negotiations that the kinds of statistical measures used by governments today to judge progress are wholly inadequate because they ignore the stock of national capital, and that new indicators need to be applied. The UN Statistical Office has already developed some indicators which incorporate environmental and resource accounting,[4] and Chapter 8 of Agenda 21 (Programme Area D) calls upon the Office 'to make available to all member States the methodologies .'., and to 'develop, test, refine and then standardize the provisional concepts such as those proposed by the SNA handbook', together with relevant training. Various other bodies are urged to assist in making such indicators operational. Chapter 40 reinforces the need to develop indicators of sustainable development and 'to promote their increasing use .. in satellite accounts, and eventually in national accounts'. Inventories and the various follow-ups targeted at generating more understanding of global resources and their degradation will add more.

---

[4] *SNA Handbook on Integrated Environmental and Economic Accounting*, UN Statistical Office, New York.

Analysts have been calling for such developments for many years; in the aftermath of UNCED, Roddick[5] suggests that 'a major sea-change in the ways we measure national performance within the international economy is on the horizon'.

A broader sea-change is the one wrought in terms of psychology and to an extent institutions at the national level. The UNCED negotiations, and all the associated processes sketched out in section 2.5, formed a global educational exercise which also required institutional innovations within and outside governments. To an extent these have persisted.

Given this, Agenda 21 may still play an important role at the national and local levels quite irrespective of international oversight. Many governments are reviewing their national policies in its light, and its emphasis on the importance of community-based actions was not borne of a vacuum; it both reflects and reinforces the interests and concerns of many different non-governmental groups, at many different levels throughout societies around the world. The ideas set out in Agenda 21 may be studied by many such groups, who will seek to contribute their own efforts, and to hold their governments accountable against the measures set out. Agenda 21 may never achieve even the status of 'soft law' suggested for the *Rio Declaration*, but that does not make it irrelevant to actions taken over the following decades. The chapters in this study on the *Rio Declaration*, Agenda 21 and the Forest Principles all give indications of the way in which these 'soft' agreements can influence behaviour, both directly and when used as levers in the hands of many and varied NGOs, acting upon their own communities and governments, and building upon the perceptual and institutional changes wrought by the UNCED process.

## 5.4 Tensions and prospects

Nevertheless, the original aim of UNCED was much grander. Besides the sweeping but generalised calls for UNCED to mark a radical change in the whole structure of development and international cooperation, even those close to the process hoped for much more than actually emerged.[6] They sought

---

[5] J.Roddick, 'The road from Rio: institutions and indicators', *SANGEC Bulletin*, University of Glasgow, Autumn 1992.

[6] A good example of specific hopes for UNCED may be found in the final chapter of the book authored by the Secretary-General of the World Commission on Environment and Development and colleagues, Jim MacNeill, Pieter Winsemius, and Taizo Yakushiji, *Beyond Interdependence*, Oxford University Press, New York, 1991.

agreement on a sweeping Earth Charter; conventions to assist development whilst containing binding and quantified commitments on greenhouse gas emissions and the preservation of species and forests; and an Agenda 21 backed with targets of achievement and agreement on associated funding requirements, mechanisms and contributions for achieving those targets.

Thus despite the substantial changes which UNCED has wrought especially in international mechanisms, it is still a very pertinent question to ask how far policies towards sustainable development can go without more specific commitments. This is a particularly serious question when the tentative advances in international institutions and processes are at best patchily reflected at the national level, and countries operate within an increasingly open international economic system, in which capital, industry and effluents (but not people) can readily migrate to avoid stricter environmental policies or other higher developmental costs. There is nothing in the UNCED agreements formally to answer this question. But much may be gleaned from the UNCED process itself and the themes which emerged, including those outlined in Chapter 4.

Beneath all the specific issues and conflicts which may arise, two general tensions seem likely to dominate. One is the North-South division. This division pervaded everything about UNCED, and little about the agreements suggests that the gulf has really been narrowed; nor do the follow-up UN General Assembly resolutions, which alongside the specific measures are replete with the stale stock phrases from years of North-South dispute in the UN. One reviewer commented that North-South relationships 'are never easy - like male-female relationships',[7] because as well as differing interests they have genuinely different perceptions of the problems and priorities. Despite some modest underlying developments (eg. in the increased acceptance of market principles), conflicts over funding levels, over the control of finance, technology, and intellectual property, and over relative responsibilities including the focus given to population or consumption levels, seem bound to persist. These and other disputes may yet politicise the new international institutions to the point of crippling them.

The other central tension is that between perceived sovereign national interest on the one hand, and international responsibilities on the other. The international institutional processes established by UNCED can only have an impact through actions within countries, and by the consent of sovereign

---

[7] J.Roddick, personal communication.

governments. Even if sustainable development is now much more firmly rooted as an important concept, on each specific issue at least some governments will have strong reasons related to their perception of short-term political and national interests for resisting the desires of the broader international community. The agreed and recognised system of specific international legal commitments, acting only upon those who agree to the relevant clauses, is one thing. Acquiescing to much more general pressures from international institutions in pursuit of the common good may be quite another. Much may thus hinge on the significance which governments choose to attach to the recommendations and criticisms from the international processes which they have now established - which will reflect on the credibility of the UN system itself.

The history of international environmental (and other) politics to date suggests that such general institutional pressures may have modest impact, in which case more substantive measures to address problems will emerge on a piecemeal basis. The more significant issues raised in Agenda 21 may be picked off one by one in further international conventions, or as protocols to existing conventions, as individual disasters, or as the cumulative impact of events, move problems up the political spectrum. It is hard to predict which environmental issues will emerge as individually important, but possibilities appear to include not only the obvious issues of desertification and deforestation, but also: broader land degradation; pollution of waterways and seas; global fish stocks; the generation and transport of various wastes (including chemical and nuclear wastes, especially plutonium); and other issues barely touched upon even in Agenda 21, such as mining practices and inner-orbit space debris. There may even be attempts to raise for legal attention the broader and highly contentious cross-cutting issues, such as population, migration and consumption patterns.

Consequently, it seems possible that future decades will herald many further conventions, each emerging only after problems become pressing, and each repeating the same underlying themes of sovereignty versus cooperation, population versus consumption, South versus North, etc. - perhaps largely cast in the pre-UNCED image of development versus environment. It must be questionable whether this is really a good way to go. The UNCED process did achieve much in the attempt to develop a broader change in perceptions and behaviour. Yet set against the high initial hopes for more specific commitments, the outcome does not suggest as yet any clear idea of a politically practical alternative approach towards the more difficult elements of sustainable development.

# PART II: THE UNCED AGREEMENTS

Chapter 6

United Nations Framework Convention on Climate Change

Michael Grubb
Energy and Environmental Programme
Royal Institute of International Affairs

## 6.1 Origins and objectives

Scientists have known for many decades that an increase in the atmospheric concentration of carbon dioxide ($CO_2$) and other gases which absorb infra-red radiation should warm the earth's surface, changing climates in various ways. Measurements started in 1957 showed unambiguously that atmospheric concentrations of $CO_2$ were rising steadily due to human activities, primarily fossil fuel burning and deforestation. Subsequent work showed that the concentrations of other such 'greenhouse gases' were also rising.

Scientific meetings in 1985 and 1987 established a broad (though not universal) scientific consensus on the nature and potential seriousness of the problem. This coincided with the general rise in environmental concerns in the late 1980s, and was brought to a head at the Toronto Conference in 1988, which coincided with a series of climate anomalies, the most important of which (though by no means the most damaging) was the US drought. Seeking a firmer scientific understanding, UNEP and the World Meteorological Office (WMO) established the Intergovernmental Panel on Climate Change (IPCC) in 1988. Over the subsequent two years the IPCC effectively conveyed the scientific issues, and brought a range of countries that had hitherto been uninterested and ill-informed into the discussions. In doing so, the work of the IPCC, together with continued public concern, established the political conditions for the start of formal negotiations.

In December 1990 the UN General Assembly took control of the negotiating process directly (unlike the ozone negotiations and the IPCC, which had been under the auspices of UNEP and WMO), and negotiations began near Washington in February 1991. The gulf between negotiators was enormous. Some were already convinced about the seriousness and urgency of the problem and wanted a convention which contained binding commitments to limit greenhouse gases. Others recognised the problem, but wanted to tread more cautiously, providing first a general legal framework, leaving any binding measures to subsequent negotiations. Some developing country participants even feared the whole issue as a conspiracy by Northern countries to impede their development, and their main instructions seemed to be to avoid any commitments.

With the UNCED conference set as a deadline, the Convention was completed in fifteen months. For such a politically complex issue, the timescale was relatively short (although political skirmishing had already begun in meetings of the IPCC Response Strategies working group). Indeed, the last session was suspended and reconvened after an interval which allowed the conference chairman, Jean Ripert, to present his own synthesis based on the mass of bracketed text left from what had originally been intended as the final meeting. This draft - which was accepted as the basis for the final negotiations - brought some coherence to the document, but it still represents a snapshot of an evolving political process, in some respects incoherent and in many details undefined or deliberately ambiguous.

## 6.2 The Convention

The preamble to the Convention serves as a set of agreed facts, covering a wide spectrum: the underlying scientific concern; the primary role of industrialised country emissions in the past; that appropriate levels of response 'should reflect the environmental and developmental context'; the 'principle of Sovereignty of States in international cooperation'; the need for continued research and measures 'continually re-evaluated in the light of new findings'; that 'various actions .. can be justified economically in their own right and can also help in solving other environmental problems'; the special concerns of low-lying countries and those 'whose economies are particularly dependent on fossil fuel production, use and exportation'.

The impression conveyed is thus one of concern, tempered by the acknowledged uncertainties and the stated precedence of national economic interest. It clearly places the emphasis on developed country action, and points towards an iterative approach which adapts to improving information and changing circumstances.

**Article 2 (Objective)** then states:

> The ultimate objective of this Convention .. is to achieve .. stabilization of greenhouse gas concentrations in the atmosphere at a level that would

prevent dangerous anthropogenic interference with the climate system. Such a level should be achieved within a time frame sufficient to allow ecosystems to adapt naturally to climate change, to ensure that food production is not threatened and to enable economic development to proceed in a sustainable manner.

The Objective thus recognises that some climate change is inevitable, but is concerned to limit the rate and ultimate extent.[1] Some considered this a relatively strong Objective, accepted rather reluctantly by some parties; depending on how the science evolves, and how the terms 'dangerous interference' and the requirement to 'allow ecosystems to adapt naturally' especially are interpreted, it may prove to be a far from trivial undertaking.

**Article 3 (Principles)** then sets out guiding principles, which echoes elements of the preamble. The Principles are something of a short wish list, some of which are either impractical if taken literally (eg. full comprehensivity) or impossible to define clearly. Delicate negotiations thus introduced the article with a Chapeau stating that 'Parties shall be guided, *inter alia*, by the following... ':

- the need to protect the climate system 'on the basis of equity and in accordance with [States] common but differentiated responsibilities and respective capabilities. Accordingly, the developed country Parties should take the lead .'..;[2]
- 'the specific needs and special circumstances of developing country Parties, especially those that are particularly vulnerable ... ' (eg the low-lying island states, and the primary fossil fuel exporters);
- the need for precautionary measures in the absence of full scientific

---

[1] This Objective is formulated much as proposed by the EC, drawing upon an earlier Ministerial Declaration from a conference at Noordwijk in November 1989.

[2] In adopting this principle, there was little dissent that developed countries should take the lead, but there were important disputes as to why. Developing countries argued that a major factor was the historical 'debt' arising from the much higher past emissions of industrialised countries, which have monopolised the available 'environmental space' of the planet. The USA argued that past emissions were a matter of history, and current generations could not be held accountable for this; the need for developed countries to take the lead was simply a reflection of their current relative wealth. This dispute is likely to resurface when attempts are made to reach agreements which require closer specification of the meaning of 'on the basis of equity....'.

certainty,[3] qualified by the need to be 'cost effective', and 'comprehensive', ie, address all sources and sinks, adaptation and all economic sectors;
- 'Parties have a right to and should, promote sustainable development .. integrated with national development programmes';
- 'Parties should cooperate to promote a supportive and open international economic system. Measures taken ... should not constitute a means of arbitrary or unjustifiable discrimination or a disguised restriction on international trade'.

The central focus of debate was upon **Article 4 (Commitments).** This finally emerged as a long and convoluted article, deliberately ambiguous in places. The first extended paragraph commits all Parties to:

- 'Develop, periodically update, publish and make available to the Conference of the Parties, in accordance with Article 12, national inventories' of greenhouse gas emission sources and sinks;
- 'Formulate, implement, publish and regularly update national and, where appropriate, regional programmes containing measures to mitigate climate change ... and measures to facilitate adequate adaptation to climate change';
- 'Promote and cooperate in the development, application and diffusion, including transfer, of technologies, practices and processes .'..;
- 'Cooperate in preparing for adaptation to the impacts of climate change; develop and elaborate appropriate and integrated plans for coastal zone management, water resources and agriculture, and for the protection and rehabilitation of areas, particularly in Africa, affected by drought and desertification, as well as flood';
- Various general aims including 'promote sustainable management', and 'promote and cooperate' in a wide range of other measures including conservation and enhancement of sinks and reservoirs of greenhouse gases; scientific, technological, socio-economic etc. research and the open and

---

[3] The full wording is: 'The Parties should take precautionary measures to anticipate, prevent or minimize the causes of climate change and mitigate its adverse effects. Where there are threats of serious or irreversible damage, lack of full scientific certainty should not be used as a reason for postponing such measures, taking into account that policies and measures to deal with climate change should be cost-effective so as to ensure global benefits at the lowest possible cost.' The clumsy language on this 'precautionary principle' draws on the difficult compromise reached between the Europeans and the USA in the Ministerial Declaration at the Bergen conference in May 1991.

prompt exchanges of relevant information; education, training and public awareness;

- 'Communicate to the Conference of Parties information related to implementation'.

The second extended paragraph commits 'developed country Parties and others included in Annex 1' to more specific measures:

a) 'Each of these Parties shall adopt .. policies and take corresponding measures on the mitigation of climate change, by limiting its anthropogenic emissions of greenhouse gases and protecting and enhancing its greenhouse gas sinks and reservoirs. These policies and measures will demonstrate that developed countries are taking the lead in modifying longer-term trends in anthropogenic emissions consistent with the objective of the Convention, recognizing that the return by the end of the present decade to earlier levels of anthropogenic emissions of carbon dioxide and other greenhouse gases not controlled by the Montreal Protocol would contribute to such modification ..'...[4]
This is qualified by '.. taking into account' the need to recognise various differing circumstances, and to 'maintain strong and sustainable economic growth', and states that 'Parties may implement such policies and measures jointly with other Parties'.

b) 'Each of these Parties shall communicate, within six months of the entry into force of the Convention for it and periodically thereafter ... detailed information on its policies and measures referred to in subparagraph a)

---

[4] The form of reference to greenhouse gases is a delicate compromise. Early in the negotiations, the USA had argued for a 'comprehensive approach' in which all greenhouse gases were considered collectively; this was argued to be more rational than considering different gases individually, since it is the impact of all gases combined which determines the radiative forcing of climate. However, by thus including CFC reductions made under the Montreal Protocol, it could then be claimed that total greenhouse gas emissions were being stabilised. Other countries strongly contested the validity of 'double-counting' credit for reductions which were being achieved primarily for other reasons, as mandated in other international agreements; and argued furthermore that it was both impractical to consider all gases together because of their fundamentally different characteristics (eg. some contributions are highly uncertain), and ultimately misleading, because $CO_2$ is projected to form the bulk of future contributions and forms the central problem. The final wording, reluctantly accepted by the USA and energy-exporting countries, is explicit in rejecting double-counting of CFC reductions under the Montreal Protocol, and partially acknowledges the others concerns about the 'comprehensive approach'.

above, as well as on its resulting projected anthropogenic emissions ... for the period referred to in subparagraph a) [ie. to the year 2000] with the aim of returning individually or jointly to their 1990 levels these anthropogenic emissions ... This information will be reviewed by the Conference of the Parties, at its first session and periodically thereafter, in accordance with Article 7';

c) '.. The Conference of the Parties shall consider and agree on methodologies for these calculations at its first session'.;

d) 'The Conference of the Parties shall, at its first session, review the adequacy of subparagraphs (a) and (b) above ... [and] take appropriate action, which may include the adoption of amendments to the commitments in subparagraphs (a) and (b) above ... A second review of subparagraphs (a) and (b) shall take place not later than 31 December 1998, and thereafter at regular intervals determined by the Conference of the Parties, until the objective of the Convention is met'.

This section further requires each of these Parties to 'coordinate as appropriate with other such Parties, relevant economic and administrative instruments.'.., and to 'identify and periodically review policies and practices which encourage .. [greater emissions] than would otherwise occur' - a pointed reference to policies such as coal subsidies. The Conference of Parties is also required to review the list of countries (Annex 1) to be covered by these commitments. This list already contains the 'transition economies' of Eastern Europe, the Baltics and the Russian Federation; a separate paragraph (6) states that 'a certain degree of flexibility shall be allowed .. to Parties undergoing the process of transition to a market economy'.

Paragraph 3 addresses financial resources and states that developed Parties (listed in Annex II - excluding the transition economies):

'shall provide new and additional financial resources to meet the agreed full costs incurred by developing country Parties' in preparing reports under the convention (Article 12), and 'shall also provide such financial resources, including for the transfer of technology, needed by the developing country Parties to meet the agreed full incremental costs of implementing measures that are covered by paragraph 1 of this Article and that are agreed [between that country and the funding agency]'.

This wording was very delicate; exactly how the term 'agreed full incremental cost' is to be interpreted, and just who has to agree and how, is a question that is already exercising the minds of experts in many different countries and in the World Bank, and is likely to be a key point of future debate.

Paragraphs 4 and 5 also commit the developed (Annex II) Parties to 'assist' particularly vulnerable developing countries to meet the costs of adaptation; and to 'promote, facilitate and finance' the transfer of technologies. Paragraph 7 then underlines the message by stating that implementation of any commitments by developing countries 'will depend upon' developed countries meeting their commitments, and will take fully into account that 'economic and social development and poverty eradication are the first and overriding priorities of the developing country Parties'.

Paragraph 8 reiterates that Parties 'shall give full consideration ... ' to meet the 'specific needs and concerns' of no less than nine specified categories of countries which may be particularly sensitive to the impact of climate change or response measures. Paragraphs 9 and 10 emphasise further the 'specific needs .. of the least developed countries'.. with respect to technology transfer, and the 'situation of Parties .. that are highly dependent on ... fossil fuels'.

The short **Articles 5 and 6** address respectively **Research and Systematic Observation**, and **Education, Training and Public Awareness**, in language which calls on Parties generally to support, develop, cooperate, promote etc. suitable measures.

**Article 7** establishes the **Conference of Parties**, which 'shall keep under regular review the implementation of the Convention and any related legal instruments ... and shall make, within its mandate, the decisions necessary to promote the effective implementation of the Convention', with a list of 13 particular sub-tasks, which require the Conference of Parties to:

- review obligations and their adequacy in the light of developing knowledge and the objective of the Convention;
- facilitate exchange of information, and the coordination of measures adopted by Parties;
- 'Consider and adopt regular reports on the implementation of the Convention and ensure their publication';
- 'seek to mobilise international resources .'..;
- prepare guidelines, methodologies, rules of procedure etc.;
- take other measures as deemed necessary, eg. establish (additional) subsidiary bodies and provide guidance to them.

The Conference of Parties is thus, in effect, charged both with sorting out all the issues which could not be resolved in the time span of the Convention negotiations, and with reviewing progress in the light of expanding knowledge and changing circumstances. It is the central body with the authority to determine what happens, when, and how. To this end, the first meeting shall take place within a year of entry into force of the convention, and every year thereafter unless otherwise decided by the Conference of Parties itself; extraordinary sessions may be held if supported by at least one-third of the Parties.

**Article 8** establishes the **Secretariat** which will deal with day-to-day running of the Convention and associated efforts, transmission of reports, and preparation for meetings of the Conference of Parties.

**Article 9** establishes a **Subsidiary Body for Scientific and Technological Advice**, which shall 'provide the Conference of the Parties and, as appropriate, its other subsidiary bodies with timely information and advice on scientific and technological matters.... This body .. shall comprise government representatives competent in the relevant field of expertise'. To this end, and 'drawing on existing competent international bodies' - a reference to the many existing international research programmes and the IPCC - it shall 'provide assessments of the state of scientific knowledge', and of the 'effects of measures taken in the implementation of the Convention'; 'identify' relevant technologies and knowledge, and advise on their promotion and transfers; and respond to question posed by the Conference of Parties and other subsidiary bodies. The relationship of this body to the IPCC remains unclear (see below).

**Article 10** establishes a **Subsidiary Body for Implementation** 'to assist the Conference of Parties in the assessment and review '.., similarly composed of 'government representatives who are experts.. '. The text is a shadow of some earlier drafts which attempted to establish a strong body required to critically review national reports; it shall 'consider the information communicated' , in ways which have yet to be clearly defined.

**Article 11**, **Financial Mechanism**, addresses the thorny issue of control of finances, and states:

1. 'A mechanism for the provision of financial resources on a grant or concessional basis, including for the transfer of technology, is hereby defined. It shall function under the guidance of and be accountable to the Conference of the Parties, which shall decide on its policies, programme priorities and eligibility criteria related to this Convention. Its operation

shall be entrusted to one or more existing international entities'.
2. '... with an equitable and balanced representation of all Parties within a transparent system of governance'.
3. 'The Conference of the Parties and the entity .. shall agree upon arrangements to give effect to the above paragraphs .'..

These reflect the central tensions underlying the negotiations. A mechanism is *defined*, not established; in relationship to the Convention it is at the service of the Conference of Parties, and yet it shall be operated by existing entities, with which arrangements on relevant modalities, eligibility criteria, and 'determination of the amount of funding necessary and available .. and the conditions under which that amount shall be periodically reviewed' have to be agreed. Article 21 defines this body on an interim basis to be the GEF of the World Bank, UNDP and UNEP; the Conference of Parties shall consider at its first session whether these interim arrangements shall be maintained.

**Article 12** specifies more closely the information to be communicated by Parties. Mostly, this shadows directly the commitments of Article 4; notably, each of the Annex 1 (industrialised) countries shall incorporate 'a detailed description of the policies and measures it has adopted to implement its commitment under Article 4', and 'a specific estimate of the effects that the policies and measures .. will have on [net] emissions'. These parties have to provide this information within six months of entry into force of the Convention; developing country Parties are given three years from the entry into force 'or of the availability of financial resources in accordance with Article 4'. Parties can designate some information in their reports to be confidential, which shall 'then be aggregated by the secretariat to protect its confidentiality'.

**Articles 13 and 14** address the resolution of implementation questions and disputes, and establish that Parties to disputes may submit to arbitration by either the International Court of Justice, or of the Conference of Parties if both desire; failing which, a conciliation commission shall be established if the dispute has not been resolved after 12 months.

**Article 15** establishes the conditions for **Amendments to the Convention:**

'The Parties shall make every effort to reach agreement on any proposed amendment to the Convention by consensus. If all efforts at consensus have been exhausted .. amendment shall as a last resort be adopted by a three-fourths majority vote '..

In which case, an amendment so adopted '... shall enter into force for those Parties having accepted it on the ninetieth day ... '. Other Parties are not bound, until they indicate acceptance. Thus, the rule of unanimity is breached, with greatest reluctance; but any such breaches shall not be binding on the dissenting Parties. The *caveat* is unavoidable, since countries cannot be bound to things they have not accepted;[5] it is a twist which prevents individual countries from blocking amendments to the Convention, leaving them instead permanently and visibly at odds with the majority.

**Article 16** establishes that **Annexes to the Convention** are an integral part of it, subject to essentially the same rules as the Convention itself. **Article 17** makes provision for **Protocols**, in five short sentences which state that Protocols may be adopted by the Conference of Parties, and should essentially be self-contained instruments bearing only upon the Parties to the Protocol concerned.

With the exception of Article 21 on Interim Arrangements, the remaining Articles address administrative details, including the role of regional economic integration organisations (the EC) as signatories, and their relationship to the Parties which comprise them. Entry into force is established by the fiftieth ratification; most observers expect this within two years at most.

**Article 21** on **Interim Arrangements** establishes the GEF as the interim funding mechanism, as noted, and states that the existing secretariat to the negotiating committee will continue until the full secretariat is established, and shall 'cooperate closely with the IPCC'; a resolution on interim arrangements annexed to the report of the Committee establishes that the existing negotiating committee will continue to meet to prepare for the first Conference of Parties.

## 6.3 Discussion and prospects

The Framework Convention on Climate Change is a complex document. In many respects, given the timescale, complexities and political obstacles at the start of the negotiations, it is a considerable achievement. It has certainly succeeded in one of the primary aims, that of providing an international legal framework and set of principles which was acceptable to almost all the countries involved. It accepts that climate change is a serious problem and that addressing it at present is primarily a responsibility of the industrialised

---

[5] The only exceptions to this in international law are the provisions for Qualified Majority voting in the EC, in which decisions are binding on Member States; and a provision in the Montreal Protocol which allows for majority voting on amendments which tighten the previously agreed schedule of reductions.

countries, given their relative wealth and the fact that they have dominated emissions; the developing countries are indeed committed to nothing unless the developed countries pay for it. A step-by-step, evolving approach based on the expectation of improving information is clearly established, with considerable emphasis both on the need to report information and to re-evaluate commitments. There is also clear emphasis that information should be open to public scrutiny.

The criticisms centre upon that fact that, despite both accepting the reality of the problem, and a 'precautionary principle' (albeit in a weak form) towards uncertain environmental impacts, there are as yet no clear commitments which will limit the growing interference with the atmospheric heat balance. The convoluted wording on emission goals in Article 4 is the outcome of the battle in which many OECD countries had been calling for a formal commitment to stabilise $CO_2$ emissions. The USA argued that such a commitment was arbitrary, unenforceable and premature; but under considerable pressure, it eventually compromised sufficiently to allow the less direct, and disjointed references which finally appeared. Legally these mean little, but politically they could prove a crucial reference point if countries use it as such, and if countries that have declared intention to reduce or stabilise emissions can stick to their commitments.

In isolation, the unquantified commitment to adopt policies which limit emissions may be deceptively ambiguous, since nearly all policy changes in the energy, agricultural and forestry sectors ultimately affect emissions; half, on average, could thus be presented as abatement policies unless this is more clearly defined. Thus, the requirement to report on abatement and adaptation policies and project their impact assumes a central role in the convention. In reality, the minimal reporting requirements could be fulfilled with little more than the studies that many countries have already produced. A great deal may thus hinge on the precedents set by the range, quality and honesty of the first few national reports, and the depth and independence of assessments provided by the Subsidiary Body for Implementation to the Conference of Parties.[6]

Also of central importance, the involvement of developing countries will depend heavily upon the money offered, how the GEF operates as the funding agency, and how the developing countries themselves approach their national studies - for which funding is already virtually guaranteed. In another sphere,

---

[6] For more detailed discussion of the reporting requirements, and potential weaknesses therein, see M.Grubb, 'The Climate Change Convention: an assessment', *International Environmental Reporter* Vol.15, No.16, 12 August 1992.

the subsidiary body for scientific and technological advice could usefully complement the work of the IPCC, acting as an interface which helps keep the IPCC clear of political interference, and which injects necessary political judgement into quasi-technical issues. Alternatively it could be distorted into a political device for undermining the IPCC, and/or otherwise shielding diplomats from awkward scientific and other analytic conclusions.

The 'commitment to revisit commitments' and see if they are adequate, with the encouragement to amend the Convention if seen fit, is another central feature. In this, it differs widely from the 1985 Vienna Convention on the Protection of the Ozone Layer, which contained no emission 'aims' at all and left all to the subsequent Montreal Protocol. The article on protocols in the Climate Convention is by contrast skeletal and unenthusiastic; it sets no timetable or structure, and diplomats differ greatly in their assessment of what protocols should or may be negotiated, and when. Some are even suggesting that protocols may never be invoked, arguing that it would be easier to make progress by amending the Convention. This has the benefit that amendment through the procedures established may be much easier than opening negotiations on a wholly new protocol text. The drawback is that the current contorted ambiguities seem a very poor starting point for developing the kind of coherent, quantified, clearly defined and monitored regime which may be required if global emissions are to be seriously curtailed. It may be that the ability to amend the Convention can buy time and experience until the political conditions exist to create such a protocol.

Thus it remains unclear how many aspects of the Climate Convention will operate in practice, and it can only be seen as an important first step on a very long road. The process of negotiating the Convention itself had an impact, both in educating many different countries, and in pushing concerned countries towards making and explaining commitments. The impact of the Convention itself will depend upon how vigorously governments pursue its spirit, as opposed to the minimal text, and how far they are prepared to use continuing meetings to clarify and strengthen the nascent regime which has been created. It shows that concern about the issue has developed, but there was not time enough for this, or the implications of further steps, to permeate through political systems to the point where governments were prepared to make more substantive commitments, in the face of strong opposition from affected parties. It is possible that the issues will now be relegated to a diplomatic backwater, but this is far from certain: the process established means that governments will have to keep facing the issue, improving their understanding, and defending their policies against criticism both from the public, and from other governments in the negotiating chambers. The Convention as it stands does not ensure substantive action, but is constructed such that it could and may well be used to.

# Chapter 7
## The United Nations Convention on Biological Diversity

Abby Munson
Global Security Programme
Cambridge University, UK

## 7.1 Historical beginnings

Biodiversity is the global composite of genes, species and ecosystems. The rapid acceleration of loss of species and ecosystem degradation has caused rising concern among scientists, policymakers, and the public. UNEP estimates there are about 30 million species on the Earth, of which only about one and a half million have ever been described, and that about one- quarter of the Earth's species risk extinction within the next 30 years.[1]

In 1987, amidst overwhelming scientific evidence of growing biological erosion, governments were called upon by UNEP to examine the possibility of establishing an international legal instrument on the conservation and sustainable use of biodiversity. The USA was the first to call for the creation of a comprehensive convention. A year later an 'Ad Hoc Working Group of Experts on Biological Diversity' was initiated by UNEP to discuss the matter. It met three times between November 1988 and July 1990. As a result of the report by the group, UNEP set up a Working Group of Legal and Technical Experts.

Two meetings later this group was transformed into the 'Intergovernmental Negotiating Committee for a Convention on Biological Diversity'. This body met five times between June 1991 and May 1992. Negotiations soon focused on an argument between countries over exchange of biological resources in return for access to technologies, particularly biotechnology. Countries with the greatest diversity of species - primarily the developing countries - insisted on sovereign rights over genetic resources within their territories, as well as access to benefits resulting from the use of such resources in the shape of biotechnology. These demands were unacceptable to certain countries, who viewed biodiversity as a common heritage of humankind, and biotechnology to be the concern of industry, and best advanced with minimal or no interference by government.

---

[1] 'The state of the global environment' cover story, *Our Planet,* Vol.4, No.2, 1992, UNEP, Nairobi, p.7.

The final draft of the Biodiversity Convention was completed on the 22 May 1992 in Nairobi, under the auspices of UNEP. The final product reflects compromise by both sides.

## 7.2 The Convention

The preamble sets the tone for the whole Convention, recognising the wide ranging implications of biodiversity conservation and use, its 'ecological, genetic, social, economic, scientific, educational, cultural, recreational and aesthetic' values. It introduces principles and criteria which underpin the understanding and implementation of the Convention: affirming that 'States have sovereign rights over their own biological resources', whilst also being responsible for 'conserving their biological diversity and for using their biological resources in a sustainable manner'; including a precautionary note by declaring that a 'lack of full scientific certainty should not be a reason for postponing measures to avoid or minimize such a threat' of significant reduction or loss of biological diversity; introducing the idea of the 'desirability of sharing equitably the benefits arising from the use of traditional knowledge, innovations and practices' of indigenous peoples relevant to conservation and sustainable use of biodiversity; and acknowledging the need for 'new and additional financial resources' and 'appropriate access to relevant technologies' for developing countries.

Unlike other conventions, such as the Convention on International Trade in Endangered Species (CITES), this Convention establishes a wider context for all biological diversity protection, as well as sustainable use of the components of biodiversity. The interdependency of the developed and the developing nations in maintaining biological diversity is recognised, as is the need for new and additional financial contributions from the developed world. Acknowledging these things make this Convention an important and successful start towards maintaining, and sustainably using biological diversity.

The **Objectives of the Convention,** set out in **Article 1,** are the 'conservation of biological diversity, the sustainable use of its components and the fair and equitable sharing of the benefits arising out of the utilization of genetic resources, including by appropriate access to genetic resources and by appropriate transfer of relevant technologies'.

Throughout the negotiations, certain governments stressed that the primary need of this Convention was to tackle biological erosion on a global scale, and that to include in the objectives matters of technology transfer and finance, would inevitably lead to the neglect of more detailed action on methods for conservation and sustainable use of biodiversity itself.

**Article 2, Use of Terms** lists definitions of terms used in the Convention, ie. biological diversity, biological resources, etc. ... **Articles 3, 4 and 5, Principle, Jurisdictional Scope and Cooperation** respectively, establish parameters of the legal scope of the Biodiversity Convention. They remind Contracting Parties that this Convention relies very much on the voluntary compliance of the nation state. Article 3, the Convention's only guiding Principle, is a direct transposition of the 1972 Stockholm Principles which acknowledges Contracting Parties' 'sovereign right to exploit their own resources', whilst ensuring such activities 'do not cause damage to the environment of other States or areas beyond the limits of national jurisdiction'.[2]

Article 4 limits each Party's obligations under the Convention to: 'areas within the limits of its national jurisdiction' and activities 'carried out under its jurisdiction or control, within the area of its national jurisdiction or beyond the limits of its jurisdiction'. Article 5 reaffirms the importance of Contracting Parties cooperating through 'competent international organisations, in respect of areas beyond national jurisdiction'.

**Article 6, General Measures for Conservation and Sustainable Use**, states that each Contracting Party:

> 'shall, in accordance with its particular conditions and capabilities, develop national strategies, plans or programmes for the conservation and sustainable use of biological diversity or adapt for this purpose existing strategies, plans or programmes which shall reflect, *inter alia,* the measures set out in this Convention relevant to the Contracting Party concerned'.

Such national plans will be crucial in the process of building up an accurate picture of existing biodiversity, conservation requirements, future sustainable uses, as well as effective coordination between nations. However, there is no requirement for governments to establish 'new' plans, and the scope and detail of national strategies, plans or programmes receives no comment. These limitations led to strong criticism from conservationists.

**Article 7**, the **Identification and Monitoring** of biological diversity and its components requires each Contracting Party 'as far as possible and as

---

[2] This Principle formed Principle 21 of the Stockholm Declaration nearly 20 years ago, and has surfaced on a number of occasions in conventions and declarations since, without appearing to have achieved much impact on national policymaking.

appropriate' to 'identify components of biological diversity important for its conservation and sustainable use', and to monitor the components of biological diversity identified 'paying particular attention to those requiring urgent conservation measures and those which offer the greatest potential for sustainable use'. This may encourage governments to neglect the conservation of those species with aesthetic or cultural value only. Also, Contracting Parties are only required to 'monitor' activities 'which have or are likely to have significant adverse impacts on the conservation and sustainable use of biological diversity'.

**Article 8,** is devoted to **in-situ conservation**, meaning conservation where genetic resources exist within ecosystems and natural habitats (or in the case of cultivated species, in the surroundings where they have developed their 'distinctive properties'). The Article is a list of initiatives which can be split into three main task areas for Contracting Parties to perform:

- straightforward conservation: establish 'protected areas' or 'areas where special measures need to be taken to conserve biological diversity'; 'regulate or manage biological resources important for the conservation of biodiversity' and 'rehabilitate and restore' degraded ecosystems;
- protection of indigenous people and their knowledge: 'subject to its national legislation, respect, preserve and maintain knowledge, innovations and practices of indigenous and local communities embodying traditional lifestyles relevant for the conservation and sustainable use of biological diversity and promote their wider application' and 'encourage the equitable sharing of the benefits';
- protection against potentially hazardous biotechnology products and exotic species: develop legislation and/or regulatory provisions to protect 'threatened species', and 'establish or maintain means to regulate, manage or control the risks associated with the use and release of living modified organisms resulting from biotechnology';

**Article 9** is devoted to **ex-situ conservation**, which is the conservation of components of biological diversity 'outside their natural habitats'. The Article stresses the need to carry out conservation in the 'country or origin', and the need for Contracting Parties to rehabilitate 'threatened species'.

**Article 10** is the **Sustainable Use of Components of Biological Diversity**. It was the subject of much heated debate between countries who perceived their immediate interests as involving use of biological resources, and those more interested in conservation. As a compromise, the Article calls for adoption of measures to 'avoid or minimize adverse impacts on biological diversity', to protect 'traditional cultural practices' - but only if 'compatible with conservation or sustainable use requirements'.

**Articles 11, Incentive Measures**, obliges each Contracting Party to establish policies which act as 'incentives for conservation and sustainable use of components of biological diversity'. This is important as it contrasts with economic incentives which have historically ignored sustainable use and conservation - such as agricultural subsidies.

**Articles 12 and 13, Research and Training,** and **Public Education and Awareness** are general, and will almost certainly receive more detailed attention at a later date, after the Convention has been ratified.

**Article 14, Impact Assessment and Minimizing Adverse Impacts**, establishes that each Contracting Party 'as far as possible and as appropriate shall introduce appropriate procedures requiring environmental impact assessment of its proposed projects' which are 'likely to have significant adverse effects' on biodiversity, with the motive of reducing such effects. The Article defers the subject of liability for damage to biological diversity for elaboration in a protocol.

**Article 15, Access to Genetic Resources**, is very important. The Article acknowledges the 'sovereign rights' of States over their natural resources, and the authority of states to determine access to their own genetic resources. The negotiations therefore established that genetic resources can no longer be viewed as a common resource. But the Article also establishes a *quid pro quo:* obligation to protect domestic genetic resources, use them sustainably, facilitate their use by others, 'and not to impose restrictions that run counter to the objectives of this Convention'.

Article 15 adds that Contracting Parties 'as appropriate' 'shall take legislative, administrative or policy measures... with the aim of sharing in a fair and equitable way the results of research and development and the benefits arising from commercial and other utilization of genetic resources with the Contracting Party providing such resources'. Acknowledging that Contracting Parties must share the benefits of any profits arising from work on genetic resources is commendable, especially in the light of disagreements on this issue. However, the Article is still vague as to what 'fair and equitable' means, due to the qualification added in the text that such policies should be agreed 'as appropriate', and that any sharing shall be on 'mutually agreed terms'. Also the obligations do not apply to Parties with ex-situ genetic material in their possession collected before the Convention enters into force.

**Article 16, Access to and Transfer of Technology**, recognises 'that technology includes biotechnology, and that both access to and transfer of technology among Contracting Parties are essential elements for the attainment of the objectives of this Convention'. Article 16 elaborates that access to, and transfer of, technology 'shall be provided and/or facilitated under fair and most favourable terms, including on concessional and preferential terms'. Some business interests fear this will be used by some countries to justify compulsory licensing of patents. However, none of the above terms such as 'fair and most favourable' have been defined so the meaning is somewhat vague, and furthermore any technology transfer agreement between Contracting Parties must 'recognise' and be 'consistent with the adequate and effective protection of intellectual property rights'. Consequently, most governments and observers judge that the Convention does not in fact pose a significant 'threat to business interests', (a concern expressed primarily by the USA).

**Article 17, Exchange of Information** states that Contracting Parties shall facilitate exchange of information 'from all public available sources'. **Article 18, Technical and Scientific Cooperation**, stresses the importance of promoting joint research programmes and joint ventures for relevant technologies.

**Article 19, Handling of Biotechnology and Distribution of its Benefits** requires 'as appropriate' each Contracting Party to provide participation in biotechnological research activities, and to promote 'priority access on fair and equitable basis by Contracting Parties, especially developing countries, to the results and benefits arising from biotechnologies based upon genetic resources provided by those Contracting Parties'. Such access is qualified by being 'on mutually agreed terms'.

Article 19 adds that Contracting Parties shall 'consider the need for and modalities of a protocol setting out appropriate procedures, including, in particular, advance informed agreement, in the field of the safe transfer, handling and use of any living modified organism resulting from biotechnology that may have adverse effect on the conservation and sustainable use of biological diversity'. The Biodiversity Convention goes further than Agenda 21 (Chapter 16) on biosafety. The Convention obliges Contracting Parties to consider the need for a protocol on biosafety, whereas Agenda 21 merely requires governments to consider the need for guidelines.

**Article 20** on **Financial Resources** declares every Contracting Party's duty to provide 'in accordance with its capabilities' financial support for national activities laid out in the Convention. It goes on to say that the 'developed country Parties shall provide new and additional financial resources to enable developing country Parties to meet the agreed full incremental costs to them of implementing measures which fulfil the obligations of this Convention and to benefit from its provisions'.

**Article 21, Financial Mechanisms**, caused controversy arose over the wording of paragraph 1 which states that:

> 'There shall be a mechanism for the provision of financial resources to developing country Parties for the purposes of this Convention on a grant or concessional basis ... The mechanism shall function under the authority and guidance of, and be accountable to, the Conference of the Parties .. the Conference of the Parties shall determine the policy, strategy, programme priorities and eligibility criteria relating to the access to and utilization of such resources. The contributions shall be such as to take into account the need for predictability, adequacy and timely flow of funds ... in accordance with the amount of resources needed to be decided periodically by the Conference of the Parties and the importance of burden-sharing among the contributing Parties'.

Placing the funding mechanism under the 'authority and guidance of' the Conference of Parties differs from the wording in the Climate Convention, which refers just to 'guidance'. Nineteen developed country governments signed a declaration after the final negotiations in Nairobi stating that Article 21 should not be construed to give the Conference of the Parties the power to decide the amount of individual contributions to be provided by the donor countries. Some governments repeated this reservation when signing the Biodiversity Convention in Rio, with additional statements to that effect. Donors are further protected from being forced into contributions they do not want to make by Article 23, which ensures the rules of procedure for the Conference of the Parties are decided by consensus. Article 39 makes the GEF the interim financial mechanism, and the GEF is likely to remain in this role given the donor countries firm support for it.

**Article 22, Relationship with Other International Conventions**, affirms that the Convention will not interfere with any Contracting Parties commitment to other international laws: 'except where the exercise of those rights and obligations would cause a serious damage or threat to biological diversity'.

The Conference of the Parties will transmit information such as national reports, carry out scientific reviews, have the mandate 'to set up protocols', as well as make 'amendments to the Convention' itself, as well as to protocols.

A Secretariat is established by the Convention to perform administrative tasks for the Conference of the Parties as well as 'coordinate with other relevant international bodies'. A Subsidiary Body on Scientific, Technical and Technological Advice is also set up to provide the Conference of the Parties with such advice as required.

The last 10 or more Articles deal primarily with institutional arrangements. These include most importantly the following: each Contracting Party must report to the Conference of the Parties on the action it has taken related to the Convention; the settlement of disputes should be by negotiation if possible, and if not Annex II sets out a procedure for compulsory arbitration; no reservations are permitted; and states should cooperate in the formulation and adoption of protocols. In Annex 1 provision is made for listing important ecosystems, habitats, species, communities, genomes and genes. This is important in the absence of a separate Article on Global Lists.

By the close of the Rio Conference, 155 governments had signed onto this Convention, which will enter into force 90 days after 30 signatories have ratified it. The Convention requires ratifying nations to meet within one year of its entry into force to establish a permanent funding mechanism. Realistically this means the Conference of the Parties is not expected to meet for a few years, given the time constraint governments face putting the Convention before their own national legislatures.

## 7.3 Limitations, controversies, and prospects

Many of those involved were cautious about the prospects for successful negotiation of a biodiversity convention given the limited time frame, and the size and complexity of the task. Given that, it was a remarkable achievement for governments to arrive at consensus on the need for a more global and comprehensive approach to conserving, and using, biological resources; on the need for new and additional finances, with developed countries making the predominant contribution; and on an agreement in principle to exchange fairly genetic resources for access to and transfer of technology.

However, the Convention is not free from criticism. Jaques Delors declared that the European Commission 'regards the Convention on Biodiversity as being too timid'.[3] UNEP's Executive Director, Mostafa Tolba stated that the negotiations had resulted in 'the minimum on which the international community can agree'.[4] The Convention clearly has not achieved a paradigm shift in

---

[3] Jacques Delors, Speech to the Plenary, UNCED, Rio, 13 June 1992.
[4] Mostafa Tolba, Speech to the Plenary, UNCED, Rio, 4 June 1992.

government policy needed to ensure immediate biological conservation and sustainable use. The Convention generalises the activities each national government should undertake but fails to set out a framework for truly international action for the conservation of species. Added to this, the language in the Convention is weak, with obligations commonly being qualified by 'as appropriate' or 'as far as possible'.

In the end game, however, the USA was the only government not prepared to commit itself to signing the Convention. President Bush protested it posed a threat to the US biotechnology industry, and put American jobs at risk. This was, he argued, due to a restrictive regulatory agenda for genetically manipulated products and a failure to protect intellectual property rights. Concerns that Articles 20 and 21 gave an unsatisfactory mechanism for control of finances, with too much power to the Conference of Parties, were also important factors in the US decision. For a while there were rumours that the UK and the Japanese governments would not sign the Convention, due both to their concerns about the financial arrangements, and a desire to avoid isolating the US government.[5] However, when it became clear that they would sign, and that no other government would support the US position, behind the scenes some members of the US delegation attempted to reach a compromise in the text of the Convention so that the USA could change its position, but to no avail.[6] There is a risk, in fact, of such isolationism backfiring in that if business transactions proceed under the terms of the Convention elsewhere in the world, the US biotechnology industry may experience isolation.

As a result of the prolonged arguments over access to genetic diversity and technology transfer, the Convention concentrated too heavily on these issues, and financing, at the expense of focusing on methods to conserve biodiversity.

The omission of an Article on the preparation of Global Lists of globally important areas and species on which to focus international attention, due to developing countries seeing these as potential threats to their sovereignty, may be a case in point. The Convention also arguably places too much emphasis on biotechnology and technological fixes as solutions to reverse the loss of

---

[5] The UK and Japanese governments did after some hesitation sign the Convention at Rio, but ratification will depend on the issues of financial control being sorted out.

[6] Divisions between some US negotiators and the White House were apparent. A leaked memo destroyed any attempt at finding compromise for the Convention. It has been suggested that those who leaked the memo hoped it would cause other countries not to sign the Biodiversity Convention, leading to developing countries retaliation and refusal to sign the Climate Convention.

biodiversity. Globe International point out the dangers in this, that it may 'create a reliance on the "diversity" created through technology which would replace the respect for the diversity found in nature'.[7]

Whilst the Convention acknowledges the importance of patent protection for modern biotechnology, it fails to give concrete protection for the cultural diversity, traditional knowledge and inventions of indigenous peoples and rural communities. Similarly, the need to preserve biodiversity in areas where humans live and rely on the local biodiversity has been played down. Paragraph (j) of Article 8 provides the only firm recognition of the importance of indigenous and local communities.

With all its limitations the Convention on Biological Diversity is still a considerable achievement. But it is best viewed as the first step in the climb of a very steep mountain.

---

[7] *Convention on Biological Diversity and UNCED Agenda 21. Conserving Biodiversity: The Human Element. The roles of biotechnology and Agriculture*, Background Report and Action Agenda, Globe International, Discussion Document, Washington DC, 5 February 1992.

Chapter 8

# The Rio Declaration on Environment and Development

Koy Thompson
Programme Director
International Institute for Environment and Development, London

## 8.1 The negotiating background

The Rio Declaration started life as the 'Earth Charter'. The vision of the UNCED Secretary-General Maurice Strong was of a short, uplifting, inspirational, and timeless expression of a bold new global ethic. But under the guidance of delegates who felt anything but uplifted and inspired, it became a distillation of many of the conflicts and political differences which infused the whole of the conference agenda.

In Nairobi at the first UNCED PrepCom session, delegates were told that the Earth Charter was to contain 'the basic principles for the conduct of nations and peoples with respect to environment and development to ensure the future viability and integrity of the Earth as a hospitable home for human and other forms of life'.

At the second PrepCom session held in Geneva, Maurice Strong laid out his ideas for the Earth Charter's relation to Agenda 21; 'Agenda 21 is envisaged as a programme of action for the implementation of the principles enunciated in the Earth Charter'. The UNCED Secretariat produced a preliminary check list of elements that might be considered for the Earth Charter, drawn from existing documents. At this point it became clear to delegates that the Earth Charter had no clear direction, and was more or less a 'free-for-all'.

The final shape of the Earth Charter was more or less determined during the third PrepCom session in Geneva. Discussions developed from a consolidated draft which included 145 proposals grouped into 17 headings. Early on, the Malaysians expressed concern that Earth Charter was too environmental and that the name and emphasis of the document should be changed to reflect development concerns. Their suggestion was to call it the 'Rio Declaration on Environment And Development'.

Lacking a strong central theme, the Earth Charter slowly became a distillation of the political and conceptual arguments dogging the North-South debate. Far from a timeless ethic, it was now a snapshot of history.

Inevitably the consolidated draft got bogged down. As is practice in the UN, the largest consensus bloc, in this case G77, submitted their own Rio

Declaration for consideration. This included statements on the sovereign right of nations to exploit their own resources, the right to development, the right of individuals to have freedom from hunger, poverty, and disease, and the responsibility of the richer countries to shoulder the greater burden of taking action on global environmental problems since they caused the problem in the first place.

While G77 emphasised development and global equity concerns, the industrialised world emphasised governance and environmental concerns. For example, key elements of the US draft included: that the declaration should be a prologue to Agenda 21 and not a separately agreed document; respect for human rights and democracy; open and free markets, but that markets should reflect full economic accounting of environmental costs and benefits; and the polluter pays principle. The Scandinavian governments added concepts of environmental security; the rights of indigenous peoples and women; access to information, administrative and judicial procedures; and full internalisation of environmental costs. The EC suggestions included greater clarity on burden sharing; linkage of unsustainable patterns of consumption and production with population policies supportive of sustainable development; environmental impact assessment; compensation for damage; participation and freedom of information; and environmental security.

During the fourth and final PrepCom in New York, it was clear that the text(s) had become unmanageable. Much as with the Climate Convention, the chairman for these negotiations (Tommy Koh) presented a synthesis, which after some discussion and modification was accepted as the final document. The resulting Rio Declaration consists of 27 short principles, summarised in Box 4. Despite fears that it would be reopened during the Earth Summit itself, due to an Arab-Israeli conflict over Principle 23, the text was finally accepted in Rio.

An important postscript to the Rio Declaration was the release by the US delegation of 'Interpretive Statements for the Record by the United States'. These 'interpretive statements' were in fact disclaimers on Principles 3, 7, 12, and 23. The US statement re-affirmed a long-standing objection to the phrase 'right to development' of Principle 3, apparently on the grounds if it were a 'right' it might be used to override other 'rights' perceived as more fundamental, such as human and civil rights. For Principle 7, the US statement rejected any interpretation which implies acceptance of any international obligations or liabilities. For Principle 12 it asserts that under certain circumstances trade measures can be used to protect the environment, and for Principle 23, in

**Box 4: The Rio Declaration on Environment and Development**

*The United Nations Conference on Environment and Development,*
*Having met* at Rio de Janeiro from 3 to 14 June 1992,
*Reaffirming* the Declaration of the United Nations Conference on the Human Environment, adopted at Stockholm on 16 June 1972, and seeking to build upon it,
*With the goal* of establishing a new and equitable global partnership through the creation of new levels of cooperation among States, key sectors of societies and people,
*Working towards* international agreements which respect the interests of all and protect the integrity of the global environmental and developmental system,
*Recognizing* the integral and interdependent nature of the Earth, our home,
*Proclaims that:*

1. Human beings are at the centre of concerns for sustainable development. They are entitled to a healthy and productive life in harmony with nature.
2. States have, in accordance with the Charter of the United Nations and the principles of international law, the sovereign right to exploit their own resources pursuant to their own environmental and developmental policies, and the responsibility to ensure that activities within their jurisdiction or control do not cause damage to the environment of other States or of areas beyond the limits of national jurisdiction.
3. The right to development must be fulfilled so as to equitably meet developmental and environmental needs of present and future generations.
4. In order to achieve sustainable development, environmental protection shall constitute an integral part of the development process ...
5. All States and all people shall cooperate in the essential task of eradicating poverty as an indispensable requirement for sustainable development, in order to decrease the disparities in standards of living and better meet the needs of the majority of the people of the world.
6. The special situation and needs of developing countries, particularly the least developed and those most environmentally vulnerable, shall be given special priority. International actions in the field of environment and development should also address the interests and needs of all countries.
7. States shall cooperate in a spirit of global partnership to conserve, protect and restore the health and integrity of the Earth's ecosystem ... States have common but differentiated responsibilities.  The developed countries acknowledge the responsibility that they bear in the international pursuit of sustainable development in view of the pressures their societies place on the

global environment and of the technologies and financial resources they command.

8. To achieve sustainable development and a higher quality of life for all people, States should reduce and eliminate unsustainable patterns of production and consumption and promote appropriate demographic policies.

9. States should cooperate to strengthen endogenous capacity-building for sustainable development ... through exchanges of scientific and technological knowledge, and by enhancing the development, adaptation, diffusion and transfer of technologies..

10. Environmental issues are best handled with the participation of all concerned citizens, at the relevant level. At the national level, each individual shall have appropriate access to information concerning the environment that is held by public authorities ... and the opportunity to participate in decision-making processes. States shall facilitate and encourage public awareness and participation by making information widely available. Effective access to judicial and administrative proceedings, including redress and remedy, shall be provided.

11. States shall enact effective environmental legislation. Environmental standards, management objectives and priorities should reflect the environmental and developmental context to which they apply. Standards applied by some countries may be inappropriate and of unwarranted economic and social cost to other countries, in particular developing countries.

12. States should cooperate to promote a supportive and open international economic system ... Trade policy measures for environmental purposes should not constitute a means of arbitrary or unjustifiable discrimination or a disguised restriction on international trade. Unilateral actions to deal with environmental challenges outside the jurisdiction of the importing country should be avoided. Environmental measures addressing transboundary or global environmental problems should, as far as possible, be based on an international consensus.

13. States shall develop national law regarding liability and compensation for the victims of pollution and other environmental damage. States shall also cooperate in an expeditious and more determined manner to develop further international law regarding liability and compensation for adverse effects of environmental damage caused by activities within their jurisdiction or control to areas beyond their jurisdiction.

14. States should effectively cooperate to discourage or prevent the relocation and transfer to other States of any activities and substances that cause severe environmental degradation or are found to be harmful to human health.

15. ... the precautionary approach shall be widely applied by States according to their capabilities. Where there are threats of serious or irreversible damage,

lack of full scientific certainty shall not be used as a reason for postponing cost-effective measures to prevent environmental degradation.

16. National authorities should endeavour to promote the internalization of environmental costs and the use of economic instruments, taking into account the approach that the polluter should, in principle, bear the cost of pollution, with due regard to the public interest and without distorting international trade and investment.

17. Environmental impact assessment, as a national instrument, shall be undertaken for proposed activities that are likely to have a significant adverse impact on the environment and are subject to a decision of a competent national authority.

18. States shall immediately notify other States of any natural disasters or other emergencies that are likely to produce sudden harmful effects on the environment of those States. Every effort shall be made by the international community to help States so afflicted.

19. States shall provide prior and timely notification and relevant information to potentially affected States on activities that may have a significant adverse transboundary environmental effect and shall consult with those States at an early stage and in good faith.

20. Women have a vital role in environmental management and development. Their full participation is therefore essential to achieve sustainable development.

21. The creativity, ideals and courage of the youth of the world should be mobilized to forge a global partnership in order to achieve sustainable development and ensure a better future for all.

22. Indigenous people and their communities, and other local communities, have a vital role in environmental management and development ... States should recognize and duly support their identity, culture and interests and enable their effective participation ..

23. The environment and natural resources of people under oppression, domination and occupation shall be protected.

24. Warfare is inherently destructive of sustainable development. States shall therefore respect international law providing protection for the environment in times of armed conflict and cooperate in its further development, as necessary.

25. Peace, development and environmental protection are interdependent and indivisible.

26. States shall resolve all their environmental disputes peacefully and by appropriate means in accordance with the Charter of the United Nations.

27. States and people shall cooperate in good faith and in a spirit of partnership in the fulfilment of the principles embodied in this Declaration and in the further development of international law in the field of sustainable development.

plain English, the understanding of the USA is that the principle implies nothing.[1] A cynical view is that the USA, like many other industrialised countries, would simply not sign on to the Rio Declaration if doing so implied any significant legislative or policy change. The interpretive statements somewhat support this view.

## 8.2 A commentary on the final Rio Declaration

**Principle 1** puts human beings as the centre of concerns for sustainable development, and contains a watered-down version of a right to a clean environment. Although fine as an emphasis on human development priorities, some feel that a serious sustainable development ethic should recognise the intrinsic value of the natural world, irrespective of its value to human beings.

The issue of sovereignty in **Principle 2** restates a real and recurrent UN concern. Few commented on the irony that a Summit devoted to shared global responsibilities, cooperation and partnership should so strongly assert sovereignty. A better formulation might have been to put sovereignty within the context of the principle of subsidiarity. In this way, a cooperative framework could have been promoted, but actions would be taken at the lowest most appropriate level, that is, at the national level. Some feel that because the UN lacks the level of political agreement that, for example, the European Community has, a principle of subsidiarity would be politically unrealistic. On the other hand, Principle 10 is to some extent a subsidiary principle.

The 'right to development' described in **Principle 3** is an important principle for the developing countries. Throughout the Earth Summit, developing countries pressed for an assurance that their basic development needs will not be compromised by the 'overdevelopment' of the industrialised countries. For example, if the richer countries have polluted the atmosphere to the extent that it threatens major climatic changes, this does not mean that developing

---

[1] This stance, strongly criticised in the media at the time, was stated as follows: 'The US does not, by joining consensus on the Rio Declaration, change its long standing opposition to the so-called "right to development". Development is not a right. On the contrary, development is a goal we all hold, which depends for its realisation on the promotion and protection of human rights as set out in the Universal Declaration on Human Rights. The US understands and accepts the thrust of Principle 3 to be that economic and development goals and objectives must be pursued in such a way that the development and environmental needs of present and future generations are taken into account. The US cannot agree to, and would disassociate itself from, any interpretation of Principle 3 that accepts a "right to development" or otherwise goes beyond that understanding.'

countries must stop developing. Most see the 'right' to development as rhetorical rather than legal. The US, as noted, later disclaimed the statement that development is a legal 'right'.

Following the non-contentious **Principle 4** concerning the integration of environment and development, **Principle 5** restates the UN commitment to cooperate to eradicate poverty, but makes two further important points. The first that eradicating poverty is an indispensable requirement for sustainable development, and the second is that sustainable development entails strong considerations of equity.

Debate on **Principle 6**, concerning the special needs of developing countries, highlighted basic differences in North-South perceptions. Developed nations argued that this principle was out of place in the Declaration since it involved the specific issues of finance and technology transfer which were addressed elsewhere in Agenda 21. The developing countries disagreed, saying that these were principles which cut to the heart of UNCED, and formed the very foundation of the new global partnership.

**Principle 7** contains the principle of 'common but differentiated responsibility'. In plain English this means that the although all nations have a common responsibility to develop in an environmentally sustainable way, a greater responsibility lies with the developed nations. This was widely interpreted to mean that, because historically the developed nations produced most of the pollution causing climate change and other global environmental problems, and because they are rich and have the most advanced technology, developed countries have a moral responsibility to help those developing countries who do not.[2] Wording which suggested that there should be particular emphasis on the need for the richer countries to address their unsustainable patterns of consumption, was toned down. The US delegation said repeatedly that it rejected any interpretation of this principle which implies US acceptance of any obligations or liabilities.

The issue of population was intended to be tackled in **Principle 8**. Since, however, many developing countries perceive the mention of 'population' as being synonymous with blaming the South, population is always couched in terms of 'demographic policies', and always balanced with the parallel responsibility of the richer countries to eliminate over-consumption.

**Principle 9** is twofold. First, it is a general endorsement of the importance of cooperation in capacity building, which will probably be the dominant theme in development assistance for the 90s. Second, it is a weakened principle

---

[2] See, however, chapter 6, footnote 2, p63.

on technology transfer. Whilst developing countries pushed for principles of concessional technology transfer, all Principle 9 gives them is 'enhancing the development, adaptation, diffusion and transfer of technologies'. It is argued by many developed nations that technology is best diffused through an open market, making concessional terms unnecessary.

The active participation of well-informed and concerned citizens in the pursuit of sustainable development was a strong theme throughout Agenda 21. **Principle 10** underscores this, with a principle which addresses the need for freedom of environmental information, and effective access to judicial and administrative proceedings including redress and remedy. This is an example of a principle which requires effective legal follow-up at a national level.

**Principles 11, 12**, and **14** address the interrelated issues of national environmental standards, trade, and the movement of 'dirty' goods and industries. The industry lobby had pushed hard for the harmonisation of environmental standards. Principle 11, however, addressed the concerns of developing countries that higher environmental and social standards would impose an unwarranted economic cost. Principle 11 therefore argues for country-specific standards. Principle 12 balances this by calling for a supportive and open international economy, and states that environmental considerations should not be used as disguised trade restrictions. An unanswered question is whether a country with genuinely high environmental standards for a product would be justified in imposing tariffs or even excluding products from countries with lower standards.

This also leaves open the question of dirty industry moving to poorer countries with lower standards. Consequently, Principle 14 calls on states to cooperate to ensure that there is no relocation of harmful activities and substances which may offset national efforts. A sizeable group of developing countries wanted an outright ban on the transboundary movement of toxic waste and other harmful substances; Principle 14 stops short of that, seeking only to cooperate to discourage or prevent relocation and transfer. Taken together, Principles 11, 12, and 14 present an ambiguous and in some part contradictory verdict on the desirability of free and unfettered international markets.

The controversial issue of liability and compensation for the victims of pollution and other environmental damage is covered in **Principle 13**. The thrust of this principle is to urge the further development of law in this area. Although it goes no further than existing commitments, some in industry fear that the tougher absolute or retrospective liability which may result from Principle 13 may put them out of business.

**Principles 15** and **16** are interpretations of the precautionary principle and a statement of the need to internalize environmental costs. Many feel that the precautionary principle is weakened by two qualifiers. The first is that nations should enact the precautionary principle 'according to their capabilities', which is a very broad opt-out. The second is the qualifier that actions arising from the precautionary principle should be 'cost effective'. There is no way of appropriately judging cost effectiveness unless environmental and social costs are included in the cost-benefit analysis. Principle 16 dealing with internalisation of environmental costs and the polluter pays principle is also heavily qualified. According to Principle 16, internalisation of environmental costs should take due regard of the public interest, and should not distort international trade and investment. There is some significance attached to Principles 15 and 16, since they are the first international statements accepting the precautionary and 'polluter pays' principles.

**Principle 17** urges the use of environmental impact assessment, which is useful but falls short of best practise, and does not move use towards improved environmental assessment which should incorporate social and participatory concerns.

**Principles 18** and **19** reflect concerns about environmental disasters such as Chernobyl. If a nation immediately confesses to a disaster which may affect neighbours (rather than letting their neighbours find out through remote sensing), then it is promised that every effort will be made to help. Principle 19 is concerned with prior information about activities which may lead to situations under Principle 18. It is a broad and imprecise principle.

**Principles 20, 21,** and **22** address a number of the 'major groups'. Principle 20 is a testament to the impressive power of the womens' lobby, as Principle 21 is to youth. Indigenous peoples, like women and youth are recognised for their vital role in environmental management and development, and states are called upon to recognise their culture, identity and interests. But by referring to indigenous peoples (which recognises the diversity, autonomy, and self-determined nature of different peoples), as 'indigenous people and their communities', Principle 22 subtly undermines their socio-political status.

**Principle 23** which referred to peoples under occupation is a straight piece of politicking between Israel and the Arab states, which nearly prompted Israel to pull out of the Summit.

In the post-Gulf War era, the USA attempted to remove any references to war. However, **Principle 24** contains the principle that warfare is inherently destructive of sustainable development. But far from condemning weapons of mass destruction or discouraging war *per se* (as Stockholm did), the principle only weakly calls for sticking to rules of the game in respect to the environment and war. This is small cheer to the hundreds of thousands of poor whose development efforts are continually undermined by others peoples' conflicts. Conversely, however, the statement in **Principle 25** that 'Peace, development and environmental protection are interdependent and indivisible', appears stronger than the Stockholm statements; the overall message is somewhat ambiguous - 'green war' or no war? **Principle 26**, on environmental disputes goes no further than existing documents, which is perhaps surprising since in many respects the whole of the Earth Summit is about environmental security.

**Principle 27** closes the Declaration by stating that 'States and people shall cooperate in good faith and in a spirit of partnership in the fulfilment of the principles embodied in this Declaration'.

## 8.3 Discussion

In the Preamble to Agenda 21, it is stated that Agenda 21 will be carried out in full respect of all the principles in the Rio Declaration. But how seriously will governments and others treat the Rio Declaration? It is certainly not hard law in the sense of being legally binding. Some governments felt that the Declaration could push forward the boundaries of what should be law. Some in business treat it very seriously, noting the tendency (for example in the EC) for soft law to be used as a lever to develop or promote binding legislation.

It seems certain that it would be a very tough struggle indeed to make the Rio Declaration any tougher or more explicit. For many the Rio Declaration was a damage limitation exercise, for others, an attempt to establish new precedents or springboards for future negotiation. It might be that the Rio Declaration will be applied and interpreted nationally, or in the case of the EC, regionally.

In its content, the Rio Declaration is far from the originally conceived inspirational Earth Charter.[3] It is predominantly socio-political in content, and not as ecological as some may have wished. It is a typical piece of UN negotiation, which some claim reduces every principle to the lowest common denominator. In other words it is not a pointer into the future, but a snapshot of history. NGOs would also have preferred a text which emphasised 'thou shalt' rather than 'thou shalt not'. At a national level, the utility of the Rio Declaration will be strongly country specific. It is the lowest common

[3] This analysis draws heavily upon Koy Thompson, *The Earth Summit Report*, UK Countryside Commission, September 1992.

denominator of negotiation. Cynics would say that for progressive nations, it is very weak, and for those who are not progressive, there are sufficient 'qualifiers' to get out of any real commitment. It will take a very committed and persistent civil society to move things forward with the Rio Declaration as a tool. Optimists will point to the spirit of participation and local action. Historians will note the Rio Declaration as a brutish distillation of the conflicts between the priorities of the rich North and the poorer South; and the tensions between self-centred nationalism and sovereignty, and the necessity for cooperation and partnership imposed by our sharing one small and threatened Earth.

Does the Rio Declaration represent progress from the Stockholm Declaration of Principles? This is not an easy question to answer, and perhaps is an inappropriate question. The Rio Declaration is different in function and emphasis, and can only be understood in the political context within which it was written. Development is the stronger theme in the Rio Declaration, whereas environment and even wildlife issues dominate in the Stockholm Principles. The spirit of what might be called 'Only One Earth' is stronger in the Stockholm Principles, and sovereignty is not mentioned until Principle 21. The Stockholm Principles have undoubtedly influenced the development of international environmental law, but whereas the emphasis was on stating the problem of environmental decline, and elaborating mechanisms to deal with it, the problems of the Rio Declaration are more to do with implementation, blame, and responsibility. A detailed comparison would end up with a very complex score-card.

Maurice Strong expressed a hope that the Rio Declaration could be developed into an Earth Charter for the 50th Anniversary of the UN in 1995, and in Chapter 39 of Agenda 21 it is suggested that states might look at the feasibility of elaborating general rights and obligations in the field of environment and development. In other words this does leave open the possibility for the development of what was originally conceived as an Earth Charter. The world will have to move a long way in the intervening three years if this is to come about.

Chapter 9

Agenda 21

Matthias Koch
Technische Universität Berlin

Michael Grubb
Royal Institute of International Affairs, London

## 9.1 The nature of Agenda 21

Agenda 21 is intended to set out an international programme of action for achieving sustainable development in the 21st Century. It seeks to be comprehensive in its scope, and to make recommendations on the measures which should be taken to integrate environment and development concerns. To this end, it provides a broad review of issues pertaining to sustainable development, including statements on the basis for action, objectives, recommended activities, and means of implementation. These are based on experience and analysis of the issues, combined with the interests of different parties, including interests brought forward by both developing and industrialised countries.

### Style and status of the document

Agenda 21 is an immense document, but it is still far from clear quite what has been created. It is not a legal agreement; governments are not required to follow each recommendation, paragraph by paragraph and line by line. This, and the fact that it was prepared through a relatively broad participatory process, allowed a different flavour to emerge from that which is typically found in international conventions. Compared with these, Agenda 21 contains far more about the nature of the problems, aims, possible approaches and desirable policies, often expressed in rather general and non-committal ways.

On casual reading, many parts of the Agenda 21 text appear either as statements of the obvious, or as a simplistic policy 'wish list'. Yet many things are 'obvious' once stated, and the elements of Agenda 21 frequently point to ways in which policy could perhaps readily be improved. A negotiated compendium of 'good' policy guidance still has some political weight, and thus in many respects, governments negotiated the text with all the ponderous care, sharp sensitivities and microscopic detail of a legal text.

Agenda 21 is perhaps best seen as a collection of agreed negotiated wisdom as to the nature of the problems, relevant principles, and a sketch of the desirable and feasible paths towards solutions, taking into account national and other interests. It stands as a grand testimony and guide to collected national insights and interests pertaining to sustainable development, against which government and other actions can and will be compared.

Agenda 21 covers several topics which are covered by the UNCED Conventions or other existing conventions. As legal instruments, clearly the Conventions take precedence, and it was intended that the Agenda 21 chapters should support the Conventions, by outlining broader approaches and helping to set a framework of ideas for implementation. In some cases this was achieved, and the Agenda 21 text goes beyond that of the corresponding convention in its scope. However, many of the tensions during negotiations on the Conventions emerged again in the debate on Agenda 21, and in such cases language from the corresponding Convention was usually adopted. With its many cross-references to other meetings, statements and agreements, Agenda 21 also serves as a useful marker for the range of activities which have already been undertaken, or which are planned, including many of the most significant outputs from events held in the run-up to Rio.

With a mandate to address almost every issue pertaining to sustainable development, with a global scope, the process leading to Agenda 21 was inevitably of Byzantine complexity. In general, the texts which served as the basis of negotiations were presented by the UNCED Secretariat. Sometimes the Secretariat largely wrote the first drafts on the basis of many and varied inputs; in other cases, whole sections of text were lifted from documents prepared for UNCED by governments or non-governmental groups, that either volunteered contributions or were commissioned to do so. Various interested governments and non-governmental groups then proposed additional or alternative texts as negotiations proceeded. Most of the final text was then honed down during negotiations at the final PrepCom, and the most difficult sections were sent for final negotiation at Rio.

Merely to have completed such an undertaking within 22 months from the first PrepCom is not a trivial achievement. In addition to the sheer breadth of subjects, Agenda 21 also faced the difficulties raised by trying to address the concerns and problems of very disparate countries, ranging from the least to the most developed (although the main focus was upon developing countries). For example, it is very difficult to propose human health measures that can apply both to areas where even basic health services have not been developed and to those where services are established but the health problems are very different.

In bringing together such disparate interests and attitudes, the process of developing Agenda 21, and UNCED itself, also served as an immense global educational exercise for those involved.

The main purpose of this chapter is simply to summarise the main content of Agenda 21, and to note key points of interpretation or dispute in each of its chapters. The concluding section then notes a number of underlying themes which recur throughout Agenda 21. These include the 'bottom-up' approach of putting the emphasis upon people, communities and NGOs; the need for 'open governance'; the importance of adequate information; the need for adequate cross-cutting institutions; and the complementarity between regulatory approaches and market mechanisms for addressing development and environmental needs. In general, Agenda 21 really does seek to integrate environment and development, and succeeds in highlighting the linkages between many different specific issues. However, inevitably some issues are absent or only weakly addressed, so that despite its very broad scope Agenda 21 cannot quite stand as a comprehensive document.

Despite its limitations, Agenda 21 represents a remarkable and unique endeavour. Whether or not it is judged successful will depend very much upon its translation into national policies, action plans, legislation and guidelines at all levels of society, and the extent to which it influences activities within the UN system and other international bodies. Agenda 21 created the UN Commission on Sustainable Development to 'oversee its implementation', but this cannot 'enforce' the agreement in any legal sense. The real impact of Agenda 21 will depend upon the extent to which national governments and all the various groups discussed in the document, from local councils and trade unions to scientific groups, business and industry, absorb and pursue the recommendations therein, influenced also by the continued efforts of environment and development groups.

## Structure of the document

Agenda 21 is a report of over 500 pages, comprising 40 chapters, organised into four sections which address the major areas of political action, ie.

- social and economic development (Chapter 1-8);
- natural resources, fragile ecosystems and related human activities, byproducts of industrial production (Chapters 9-22);
- major groups (Chapters 23-32); and,
- means of implementation (Chapters 33-40).

Of these, the 13 chapters of the second section occupy almost half the total volume of Agenda 21. Each chapter focuses on a distinct issue, eg. poverty, freshwater, indigenous communities, legal instruments. Various programme areas in each chapter concentrate on particular problems of concern. The programme areas are generally structured as follows:

- The **Basis for action** addresses the background of concern, discusses efforts yet to be undertaken and problems which still persist.
- The **Objectives** section summarises the main issues to be addressed, and outlines the general themes to be implemented. Usually these do not set targets, but for some areas, including health and freshwater, specific goals were adopted.
- The **Activities** section outlines a variety of specific measures that the relevant bodies 'should' undertake.[1]
- The **Means of implementation** section concludes by outlining the information, resources and institutional requirements for implementing the programme area. This is usually subdivided into the following aspects:
  - i)   financial and cost evaluation: the costs for each programme area as estimated by the UNCED secretariat (see Appendix 1);
  - ii)  scientific and technological means: the need for further research and pilot projects, transfer of technology and sharing of expertise, as well as seminars and conferences to be undertaken;
  - iii) human resource development: generally expresses concern about the lack of skilled personnel particularly in developing countries and addresses the strengthening of training opportunities and education programmes;
  - iv)  capacity-building: the need for institutional and technical capacities especially in developing countries, including aspects such as policies and administration, organisational structures, institutional and legal mechanisms, international cooperation and national coordination.

---

[1] The phrasing used to introduce these activities generally takes the form: 'Governments at the appropriate level/Governments/States, with the support of / with the assistance of / in cooperation with .. relevant United Nations bodies / international and regional organisations / intergovernmental and non-governmental organisation / private sector, [sometimes adding: where appropriate / in accordance with .. ] should ...' The reason for different forms of phrasing is frequently unclear, but the general message is that the bodies addressed 'should' undertake the programme activities then set out.

This structure is not always adopted, and sometimes overlaps or inconsistencies seem to have been unavoidable.

Financial issues permeated all the negotiations, being considered the crucial factor for the implementation of Agenda 21. Initially it was hoped that the funding mechanisms, including detailed proposals for the financial requirements of each programme area, could be negotiated, but this proved impossible. Instead, the estimates provided by the UNCED Secretariat were noted at the end of each programme area, together with a strong *caveat* indicating that these were 'indicative and order of magnitude estimates only and have not been reviewed by Governments'. These estimates, which were never scrutinised during negotiations, are summarised in Appendix 1 to this report, as is the actual funding situation, at the time of going to press.

**The Preamble**
The Preamble to Agenda 21 (Chapter 1) differs from the form adopted for legal documents; it serves more as a conventional introduction, allowing for general observations concerning expectations for the document, and *caveats* concerning it. The opening remarks outline the fundamental perceptions and goal of the exercise:

> 'Humanity stands at a defining moment in history. We are confronted with a perpetuation of disparities between and within nations, a worsening of poverty, hunger, ill health and illiteracy, and the continuing deterioration of the ecosystems on which we depend for our well-being. However, integration of environment and development concerns and greater attention to them will lead to the fulfilment of basic needs, improved living standards for all, better protected and managed ecosystems and a safer, more prosperous future. No nation can achieve this on its own; but together we can - in a global partnership for sustainable development'.

The Preamble reflects the complexity of addressing both environmental and developmental issues as a single overall objective. There is concern on the one hand about the devastating social and economic situation in many developing countries and on the other hand about the worsening perspective of the global environment.

The Preamble cites the 1989 UN enabling resolution (44/228) on the need to integrate environment and development concerns. To this end 'Agenda 21 addresses the pressing problems of today and also aims at preparing the world for the challenges of the next century. It reflects a global consensus and political commitment at the highest level on development and environment cooperation'.

The responsibilities and modalities are clearly established: 'Its successful implementation is first and foremost the responsibility of Governments. National strategies, plans, policies and processes are crucial in achieving this'. These shall be 'supported and supplemented' by international agencies, primarily the UN, and other international, regional and sub-regional organisations; and the 'broadest public participation and the active involvement of the non-governmental organizations and other groups should also be encouraged'.

The negotiations emphasised the deep concerns of developing countries about their economic situation in general, and the present net outflow of financial resources from the South to the North. They fear that their gloomy development perspective might even further be threatened by international environmental agreements, unless the international economic situation changes fundamentally. Consequently:

'The developmental and environmental objectives of Agenda 21 will require a substantial flow of new and additional financial resources to developing countries, in order to cover the incremental costs for the actions they have to undertake to deal with global environmental problems and to accelerate sustainable development'.

The 'new and additional' phrasing reflects the concern of the South that scarce development aid might only be redirected from existing overseas aid budgets to international environment funds. The cost estimations of the UNCED secretariat are noted as 'an indicative order of magnitude assessment, further examination and refinement is needed' (see Appendix 1).

The Rio Declaration is taken as providing guiding principles for Agenda 21: 'Agenda 21 ... will be carried out ... in full respect of all the principles contained in the Rio Declaration on Environment and Development'. In fact, this sentence was inserted primarily as a compromise designed to avoid disputes in Agenda 21 over references to the rights of 'people under occupation', but it has far broader implications.

Two additional *caveats* received special mention. The situation of East European and CIS countries ('economies in transition') is recognised in terms of 'particular circumstances', for which 'special attention' is needed. Also, the insistence of several oil-exporting Arab countries led to the addition that 'environmentally sound' always means 'environmentally safe and sound' -

phrasing long understood as reflecting caution towards nuclear power. Both these elements of the Preamble were inserted at a very late stage, as a way of avoiding repetition of the corresponding contentious phrases throughout Agenda 21.

Thus, except in its brevity, the Preamble sets the tone for Agenda 21 itself: an ungainly compromise, with specific *caveats* for special concerns and interests; but one which nevertheless usefully defines the context, and clears the political path, for agreement on the subsequent 500 pages.

In the following review, the main issues of each chapter and its programme areas are summarized, drawing mainly on 'basis of action', 'objectives' and 'activities'. Themes of the different **programme areas** are indicated in **bold**. Interpretations are based on discussions with those involved, and the limited published or draft documents available at the time of writing.[2] The main aim is to present a short distillation of the text, with brief comments on each chapter appended.

## 9.2 Section 1: Social and economic dimensions

CHAPTER 2: INTERNATIONAL COOPERATION TO ACCELERATE SUSTAINABLE DEVELOPMENT IN DEVELOPING COUNTRIES AND RELATED DOMESTIC POLICIES

*Summary*: To implement a global partnership, international cooperation and solidarity is needed, including 'a more efficient and equitable world economy'. Major obstacles for developing countries should be resolved: debt burdens, enhanced development aid and reversing the net financial flow from South to North, trade barriers, commodity prices and terms of trade. A more favourable international economy should support national efforts for sustainable development.

All countries, particularly developing countries, would benefit from 'an open, equitable, secure, non-discriminatory and predictable multilateral **trading system**', to which the first programme area is devoted. Tariff and non-tariff impediments should be removed to allow developing countries access to

---

[2] Notably, those referenced in Chapter 2, footnote 16, p8. Also, the UNCED Deputy Secretary-General gave a brief assessment of UNCED and Agenda 21 ('The Outcome of Rio', *Network '92*, No.18, June-July 1992, Centre for Our Common Future, Geneva) which also emphasises its achievements as 'a global consensus, not of experts but of Governments'.

markets for their export goods, opportunities can be seen particularly for agricultural products. Declining commodity prices have reduced export earnings. In the future, developing countries should be assisted to adopt appropriate commodity policies, international agreements for commodity markets are supported. Diversification of export markets should be strengthened. The efforts of the Uruguay Round of the GATT talks on trade liberalisation are supported.

By enhancing competition and a more efficient use of resources, open international trade is considered as supportive to environmental protection. National and international environmental policies 'should address the root causes of environmental degradation so as not to result in unjustified restrictions on trade'. **Trade and environment** should be made **mutually supportive** (second programme area). The role of multilateral fora such as GATT, UNCTAD etc. in dealing with trade and environment should be clarified.

Adequate **financial resources** should be provided to developing countries. Investment should be enhanced to achieve economic growth and to fulfil basic needs, but favourable conditions for private foreign investment are required. The indebtedness of developing countries and their heavy repayment burdens undermined their own development activities, so debt reduction schemes are needed. Additional funding for developing countries is needed 'and the efficient use of such resources are essential'.

In some countries, **macroeconomic policies** hindered efficient use and mobilisation of resources and private entrepreneurship; mismanagement and corruption are obstacles to sound administration. Economic and social policies and management practices are to be reformed to 'promote efficient planning and utilization of resources for sustainable development'. Also, 'Structural adjustment programmes... are necessary... [but] in some cases they have resulted in adverse social and environmental effects,... It is important to ensure that [they] do not have negative impacts on the environment and social development'. Fiscal policies in all countries need to be disciplinary. Generally a 'balance between production for domestic and export earnings' should be promoted, while export earnings should be improved and import substitution reduced.

*Comment: This chapter presents something of a 'wish list' on some of the most complex and long-standing difficulties underlying the North-South divide. The chapter has a strong commitment to a free international trading system, a moderate attitude towards export orientation and structural adjustment programmes. It is consistent with existing norms but serves to establish some issues explicitly. Discussions on debt primarily support existing debt strategies, which have had limited success in resolving this vast problem. At Rio, the USA sought to put more emphasis upon the importance of domestic economic policy in developing countries, and on the need to utilise available international resources efficiently, succeeding mainly in the latter. The emphasis in favour of trade liberalisation was strongly criticised by many NGOs.*

## CHAPTER 3: COMBATING POVERTY

The eradication of **poverty** is a matter of urgency, the objective of the single programme area in this chapter should be '**to enable the poor to achieve a sustainable livelihood**'. It is to be addressed at local, national and international level. Developmental policies should not undermine the conservation of natural resources and vice versa. Anti-poverty strategies should integrate poverty, development and environment and should focus on human development, to generate employment and income. Health, education and population issues should be addressed. Local communities are to be empowered and the role of women, youth and indigenous people should be recognised and strengthened. Programmes should address local needs and should be 'geographically and ecologically specific'. It should include immediate measures for the eradication of poverty as well as long-term strategies to improve the conditions for the most disadvantaged.

*In addressing the need to eradicate poverty and hunger, this is a more 'bottom-up', community-based approach than previous texts on the subject, which stresses the need to manage natural resources sustainably taking into account those who depend upon them for their livelihoods. It reflects successful NGO lobbying on the need for such an emphasis, including the impact of womens' caucuses in strengthening references concerning the role of women.*

## CHAPTER 4: CHANGING CONSUMPTION PATTERNS

'**Unsustainable patterns of production and consumption**, particularly in industrialised countries', are considered as 'a matter of grave concern, aggravating poverty and imbalances'. Measures 'must take fully into account the current imbalances in the global pattern of consumption and production'. The current consumption imbalance should be addressed to allow the provision of basic needs for all and to reduce pollution. 'A multi-pronged strategy [is required] focusing on demand, meeting the basic needs of the poor, and reducing wastage and the use of finite resources in the production process'. Our knowledge on consumption patterns is considered to be poor, its implications and its context to economic growth and population dynamics should be better understood. All countries should promote sustainable consumption patterns, but industrialised countries should implement this primarily.

Consequently, there is a need to develop **national policies and strategies to encourage changes in unsustainable consumption patterns** at various levels: industry and households as well as governments. Improved production efficiency is needed to reduce energy and material use and to minimise the generation of waste. Domestic policies to 'encourage a shift to more sustainable patterns of production and consumption' are needed. To allow the developing countries to address these problems, transfer of environmentally sound technology is to be encouraged, including new and renewable energy sources, recycling etc. Sound prices reflecting environmental costs, public awareness programmes and government procurement should be addressed.

*This chapter, which during negotiations was strongly linked with the following chapter on population, reflects the first official international recognition that the consumption patterns (and by implication life styles) of the rich are an important concern, for reasons of both international environmental impact and wealth distribution. This theme was resisted particularly by the USA, and such references were considerably toned down during negotiations. NGOs varied greatly in the extent to which they were prepared to promote language reflecting these underlying concerns.*

## CHAPTER 5: DEMOGRAPHIC DYNAMICS AND SUSTAINABILITY

'The growth of world population and production combined with unsustainable consumption patterns places increasingly severe stress on the life-supporting capacities of our planet'. Consequently, the chapter focuses on our knowledge of the links between population and sustainable development, national policies for integration of demographic issues into sustainable development, and their implementation at local level.

Population and demographic trends and factors **interact with social, economic and environmental issues**, their relationship is 'synergistic'. Human activities affect the environment, and environmental changes result in changes of population. Policies for sustainable development should address human dimensions as central matters as well as linkages towards technology and resources; their approach should be 'comprehensive'. Of particular concern for human and demographic development are large cities, while people in most vulnerable areas should also be addressed with priority. Our knowledge of the relationships among demographic dynamics, technology, cultural behaviour, natural resources and life support systems should be improved. Information on population and related issues is not always available, its awareness, particularly for decisionmakers, should be strengthened; analytical work focusing on environment and development should incorporate population matters.

Population matters affect social situation and human well-being heavily. The consequences of demographic trends on environment and development should be assessed at the **national level**. National development effort should incorporate environment and population issues and should address basic needs with priority, ie. health, education, status of women, income and employment generation. Communities should be empowered and municipal efforts should be strengthened. 'National planning policy and decision making processes should [fully integrate] population concerns'. Policies should recognise local and regional conditions and the special needs of indigenous people. With regard to demographic policies, the role of women should be strengthened and their rights fully recognised. Measures undertaken should be reported to the International Conference on Population and Development in 1994.

Integrated sustainable development programmes including population measures should be implemented on a **local level**. These programmes should address the specific needs of the people and should 'ensure sustainable use of natural resources; improve the quality of life of the people and enhance environmental quality'. 'Governments should... ensure that women and men have the same right to decide freely and responsibly on the number and spacing of their children... to enable them to exercise this right in keeping with their freedom, dignity and personally held values taking into account ethical and cultural considerations'. Comprehensive health care, particularly reproductive health care, are to be established and strengthened, relevant information material should be developed 'consistent with national priorities'. Addressing the special needs of women is crucial in an integrated population programme, and opportunities, rights, employment, and decisionmaking should be improved.

*Many commentators complained strenuously about a failure to address population issues at UNCED. The opening sentence quoted above forms the strongest statement on the desirability of curtailing population growth. However, some specialists on the subject were pleased with the emphasis on the need for community-based measures that actually affect reproductive choice, notably the central role of women's involvement and education, as being ultimately more effective than grand calls for population limits and reproductive targets. The chapter was the focus of intensive and sometimes bitter negotiations during the PrepComs, where it was partially tied to progress on Chapter 4, but it arrived in Rio just about bracket-free. During prior negotiations, the Holy See and the Philippines lobbied successfully to weaken the language on family planning and to remove any remarks on contraceptives.*

## CHAPTER 6: PROTECTION AND PROMOTION OF HUMAN HEALTH

Health interacts strongly with social economic and environmental factors. Measures should emphasise community-based approaches, should include preventative programmes and should, overall, be coordinated by 'an appropriate international organisation, such as the World Health Organisation (WHO)'.

The overall objective is 'to achieve health for all by the year 2000'. **Primary healthcare** should address the needs of the rural population with priority, their health service coverage should be improved. Basic health infrastructure is to be provided, relevant research and methodology are to be strengthened. The related areas of food as well as water supply and sanitation should be included in an overall health strategy. Development of health issues is linked to 'social, economic and spiritual development'. Citizens as well as health-related and non-health related organisations should be involved in health matters.

**Communicable diseases** remain a problem, many are related to inappropriate or non-existing water supply and sanitation. The underlying environmental issues should be addressed. HIV is likely to have infected 30-40 million people by the year 2000, with devastating social and economic consequences. National action plans should implement efforts to combat communicable diseases. Goals are set or reaffirmed for reducing or eliminating a large variety of specific diseases mainly by the year 2000. These goals should be achieved through a range of measures: improved public health and primary healthcare, education and research.

The health needs of **vulnerable groups**, ie infants, youth, women, indigenous people, and the very poor, should be emphasised. Children and youth, elderly, disabled are particularly vulnerable to health problems, eg. birth related diseases, environmental pollution, exploitation, urban problems. The goals of the World Summit for Children (UNGA: A/45/625) are recognised and supported. Efforts to improve the health situation of women should be strengthened; comprehensive health infrastructure for women, including women-centred and women-managed services, should be promoted on a comprehensive basis, and in particular their reproductive health should be improved. The disadvantage of indigenous people with regard to health and social issues should be addressed, their community initiatives and traditional knowledge should be strengthened.

The specific factors of **urban areas**, including environmental problems, poor housing and infrastructure, should be addressed. The health situation of the urban population is still badly affected. As a global objective, by the year 2000, health indicators are to be improved by 10 to 40 %, including infant and maternal mortality, accidents and other health problems. Related areas should be improved similarly, and urban health capacities should be strengthened.

**Environmental pollution** affects 'the health of hundreds of millions of people adversely'. The WHO clearly established 'the interdependences among the factors of health, environment and development', but 'most countries are lacking such integration'. Pollution abatement measures and environmental standards should be implemented. Goals to implement measures by the year 2000 in all countries were set: incorporation of environment and health in national development programmes; activities 'for providing environmental injury, hazard surveillance and the basis for abatement'; integrated programmes on pollution abatement. Urban and indoor air pollution, water pollution, pesticides, solid waste, human settlements, noise, radiation, industrial production, injury, research and monitoring should be addressed.

*This chapter focuses upon the need for inter-sectoral efforts which address health in the context of environmental and socio-economic improvements. On most of the programme areas there was not much controversy, but religious disputes (Islamic and Catholic) did arise especially over references to women's health as affected by issues of women's rights and reproductive choices.*

## CHAPTER 7: PROMOTING SUSTAINABLE HUMAN SETTLEMENT DEVELOPMENT

Because of insufficient expenditure and investment in the development of human settlements, conditions are deteriorating. Activities should focus on an 'enabling approach' by addressing participatory means and empowering of communities and groups, environmental implications should be reorganised and integrated, 'with high priority being given to the needs of the urban and rural poor, the unemployed and the growing number of people without any source of income'.

'Safe and healthy **shelter**' is to be provided for all. While adequate shelter is recognised as a basic human right, 'at least 1 billion people do not have access' to this. The Global Strategy for Shelter to the Year 2000 is supported, but further measures are needed. Particularly for the deprived urban and rural poor, immediate action should be undertaken. Access to land and financial schemes should be provided.

**Human settlement management** should be improved. The sustainable management of urban settlements should address how 'to improve the living conditions of residents, especially the marginalized and disenfranchised'. The effort of UNDP/World Bank/UN Centre for Human Settlements (Habitat) Urban Management Programme should be strengthened. Measures should adopt urban management guidelines and 'innovative city planning strategies', the role of intermediate cities in the rural hinterland should be strengthened.

Adequate land resources should be provided for all households, particularly the poor. 'Conflicting demands of industry, housing, commerce, agriculture, land tenure structures and the need for open space' make the access to land demands even more difficult. The degradation of marginal and ecologically sensitive land are of particular concern in rural areas. To address these problems adequately, land resource **planning and management** should be adopted primarily at national level, the goal being to balance human requirements and ecological needs. Planning activities should be strengthened through national plans, land resource inventories and information systems. Specific measures on land-resource management include improved national legislation, fiscal incentives and cooperation of public, private and community sectors; further coordination among international and regional agencies is supported. Appropriate measures to secure land tenure and to 'promote access to land by the ... poor' should be undertaken.

**Environmental infrastructure** includes water supply and sanitation, air and solid wastes, and is linked to a variety of other areas. 'Adequate environmental infrastructure facilities [are to be ensured] in all settlements by the year 2025'. It should be approached in an integrated manner 'through adequate pricing policies, educational programmes and equitable access mechanisms..'.. National action in developing countries should focus on building the relevant capacities to achieve the integratory approach by the year 2000. Specific measures are needed to improve the situation in informal settlements.

Sustainable **energy and transport systems** should be provided for human settlements, in particular energy-efficient technology, renewable energy sources and reduced pollution levels. In developing countries, the increasing energy needs should be addressed *inter alia* through forestry programmes for sustainable use of biomass energy and national energy programmes. Adequate urban transport planning is needed, strengthening public transport systems and non-motorised transport.

Because **disasters** cause great damage, adequate pre-and post-disaster measures should be undertaken. The overall goal is 'to mitigate the negative impact of natural and man-made disasters on human settlements, national economies and the environment'. The International Decade for Natural Disaster Reduction (the 1990s: UNGA 44/236) is recognised. A 'culture of safety' is to be promoted, including early warning systems and natural disaster research. Pre-disaster planning includes technologies and materials to reduce risks as well as training programmes.

The **construction industry** has an important role in national sustainable development by 'providing shelter, infrastructure and employment', but negative effects on environment and health should be reduced. Measures should strengthen local and small-scale activities, the use of indigenous material and employment generation.

**Human resource development and capacity-building** should be promoted 'by enhancing the personal and institutional capacity of all actors, particularly indigenous people and women, involved in human settlement development'. Traditional practices of indigenous people should be strengthened. International assistance should help to improve the national activities by the year 2000 'substantially'.

*This large chapter outlines the specific measures for the 'local Agenda 21' to be planned and implemented by local authorities. Many of the drafts were provided by the UN Committee on Human Settlements. This rather cross-*

*sectoral theme touches many other chapters of Agenda 21, eg. atmosphere, water, consumption patterns etc. The negotiations went on relatively easily, no substantial brackets were left for Rio.*

## CHAPTER 8: INTEGRATION OF ENVIRONMENT AND DEVELOPMENT IN DECISIONMAKING

The separation of economic, social and environmental issues is an important obstacle for **sustainable development policies.** A restructuring or adjustment of decisionmaking is needed by integrating socio-economic and environmental considerations. This is to be implemented at all levels, and political processes and structures should be improved to address long-term and cross-sectoral considerations and to allow continuous adjustment for future problems. National sustainable development strategies should be adopted. National activities should be reviewed and a very broad participatory approach adopted. 'New forms of dialogue' between government and various groups, particularly for women and local communities, should be implemented, including transparency, accountability of policies and access to information.

Integrated approaches to sustainable development need 'appropriate legal and regulatory policies, instruments and enforcement mechanisms' at various levels, country specificity and self-determination of priorities are to be recognised. Also, '... it is essential to develop and implement integrated and enforceable and effective laws and regulations ... based upon sound social, ecological, economic and scientific principles'. A **legal framework** for sustainable development should 'not only [act] through "command and control" methods, but also as a normative framework for economic planning and market instruments'. It should include enactment and enforcement measures, to promote compliance and to dissuade non-compliance. Some countries may need assistance for development and implementation of the framework, which should be provided internationally, on request. Inventories and reviews could be feasible during preparatory work. Countries should assess their laws on environment and development regularly, follow-up measures should be monitored.

**Market incentives and economic instruments** should be applied within a legal and regulatory framework. Market-oriented approaches 'play a complementary role ..'., 'a more effective and widespread use' of them is proposed. Fundamental objectives should include 'the incorporation of environmental costs in the decisions of producers and consumers, to reverse the tendency to treat the environment as a "free good" and to pass these costs on to other parts of society, other countries, or to future generations'. Thus, prices should come to 'appropriately reflect the relative scarcity and total value of resources and [help prevent] environmental degradation'. Governmental activities should re-orient towards an 'effective combination of economic, regulatory and voluntary' measures, reduction of subsidies, appropriate pricing policies etc. to direct towards sustainable development. Here, assistance and support for developing countries and economies in transition is needed. Training and education should include economic issues of sustainable development. Research on economic incentives should be encouraged.

The environment has yet to be included in economic accounting, appropriate **integrated environmental and economic accounting** should be developed and applied. Here, unremunerated activities should be recognised, eg. domestic work and child care. International cooperation and standardisation of these accounting systems should be enhanced. At national level, the collection of relevant data should be improved and these accounting methods should be introduced and established.

*In setting out the general measures and form of policies which need to be adopted in pursuit of sustainable development, this little-publicised chapter - finalised at PrepCom IV - forms potentially one of the most powerful of all individual chapters in Agenda 21. It stresses the need for effective policy dialogue and better economic-environmental indicators, and for a balance between regulatory and market instruments for promoting environmental goals. It reflects a strong move towards consideration of economic instruments for environmental policy, and comes very close to a global endorsement of a 'polluter pays principle'. Whilst raising the status of economic instruments, it places these firmly as complementary to regulatory and other approaches, rather than an alternative, and emphasises the need to learn more about the practical issues raised. Much of this reflected US proposals, as did emphasis upon the need to strengthen enforcement of legal instruments. Scandinavian proposals to introduce UNCTC work (see section 4.6) on formal environmental accounting for transnational corporations were not adopted.*

## 9.3 Section II: Conservation and management of resources for development

CHAPTER 9: PROTECTION OF THE ATMOSPHERE

Protection of the Earth's atmosphere involves a variety of environmental issues. International agreements on ozone depletion and climate change are recognised, additional measures of governments are supported. Activities should be integrated into socio-economic development plans.

A better **understanding** of the interactions between biogeochemical processes, human activities and the Earth's atmosphere is needed. Research should seek to reduce these uncertainties, through systematic observations and impact assessments etc.; scientific methodologies should be developed and relevant research capacities strengthened.

To promote sustainable development with regard to air pollution and greenhouse gas emissions, the following sectors should be addressed: energy, transportation, industry and terrestrial and marine resources.

- The **energy** sector needs improved energy efficiency; implementation of environmentally sound energy systems, particularly new and renewable energy sources; transfer of relevant technologies; and, appropriate energy planning and policies.
- **Transport** systems should be developed which are safer, cost effective, more efficient and less polluting; the information base on environmental issues of transport systems should be strengthened; and, an integrated approach to transport, human settlement and environmental planning should be adopted.
- **Industrial development** should undertake measures to minimise emissions into the atmosphere and industrial pollution by development and transfer of relevant technologies and adoption of impact assessments.
- **Terrestrial and marine resources** are important sources and sinks of atmospheric gases, they should be managed sustainably and conserved. Appropriate land-use practices and management of marine resources should be adopted.

The anthropogenic depletion of the **stratospheric ozone layer** caused by emissions of CFCs and halons is of growing international concern. The Vienna Convention and the Montreal Protocol should be ratified and implemented. In particular, the efforts to support developing countries and promote research on alternatives to CFCs should be strengthened. The implications of stratospheric ozone depletion, ie. health and environmental effects, should be investigated and remedial measures against additional UV radiation at the Earth's surface should be undertaken.

**Transboundary air pollution** still lacks monitoring of and information on its effects; observation systems and assessments should be strengthened. The UN ECE Convention on Long-range Transboundary Air Pollution and its programmes are supported, activities should be enhanced and agreements in other regions established. Strategies to reduce air pollution emissions should be developed and relevant technologies applied. Transboundary effects of accidents and disasters should be assessed, and early-warning systems and response mechanisms installed.

*This highly controversial chapter was the last to be resolved at Rio, excepting the chapter on finance. Argentinian proposals on international compensation for damage caused by ozone depletion were not accepted, nor were US proposals concerning the substitution of CFCs by HCFCs. A subsection on 'life styles and consumption patterns' was eliminated. The central disputes however concerned energy. Recommendations prepared for UNCED by the Committee on the Development and Utilization of New and Renewable Sources of Energy (A/CONF.151/PC/119 and A/AC.218/1992/5), were mostly ignored or greatly weakened, with the central opposition coming from the Arab group led by Saudi Arabia and Kuwait. These countries strongly opposed text supporting the promotion of energy efficiency and renewable energy, and insisted on the addition of the paragraph on 'environmentally sound' to be understood as 'environmentally safe and sound' in the Preamble (see p. 102). However, many general references to the need to promote energy efficiency and renewable sources remained, and after the final negotiations, Saudi-Arabia still placed reservations to this chapter.*

## CHAPTER 10: INTEGRATED APPROACH TO THE PLANNING AND MANAGEMENT OF LAND RESOURCES

'Land is a finite resource'. The planning and management of land resources needs to be approached in an integrated manner, ie. coordination of sectoral activities, integration of environmental, social and economic factors and consideration of various environmental compartments. Land should be provided to achieve the 'greatest sustainable benefits'. Land-resource policies should focus on 'the best possible land use and sustainable management of land resources', ie. to review the legal framework, to adopt economic instruments and institutional mechanisms, to strengthen local decisionmaking. Planning and management systems should establish an overall framework of both environmental and developmental goals; the environmental compartments should be integrated and indigenous and traditional knowledge recognised.

The following specific targets on land and land resources were set: policies should adopt 'the best possible use ... and the sustainable management ..'. by 1996 or earlier; planning, management and evaluation systems should be implemented by 2000 or earlier; institutions and coordinating mechanisms should be strengthened by 1998 or earlier; participatory measures in decisionmaking processes, particularly at local level, should be established by 1996 or earlier. Appropriate planning and management tools should increasingly be applied, ie. land data analysis and interpretation systems, impact assessment techniques and accounting methods. Public awareness campaigns on integrated land resource management should be established, public participation in policy-making should be encouraged. Information systems on land use and management should be strengthened, ie. systematic observation and assessment, data collection, community-managed systems and coordination of sectoral systems. Regional cooperation and exchange of information on land resources should be strengthened.

*The land resources chapter was accepted without difficulties, since it focused upon decisionmaking tools and structures for maximising the total sustainable benefits extracted from land, and avoided the highly political issues of land ownership and distribution.*

## CHAPTER 11: COMBATING DEFORESTATION

'... the multiple ecological, economic, social and cultural roles' of all types of forests should be recognised and supported. Activities in both developed and developing countries should concentrate on 'the management, conservation and sustainable development of forests' and on 'the sustainable utilisation and production of forests goods and services'. Implementation of appropriate forest policies requires skilled personnel, institutions and administrative capacities should be strengthened. Forest programmes should be developed, implemented and reviewed. The participation of a wide range of groups and public awareness and education should be promoted, eg. by improving the availability of information. Data systems and its linkages, information on land use, forest cover, ecological values as well as international cooperation on sustainable forest management should be promoted.

**Protection, sustainable management and conservation** of all forests needs urgent action. In degraded areas, forests should be rehabilitated. The 'ecological, biological, climatic, socio-cultural and economic contributions of forest resources' are recognised; the programme Objective is 'to maintain existing forests through conservation and management, and sustain and expand areas under forest and tree cover, in appropriate areas of both developed and developing countries'. National action programmes should be established, such as under the Tropical Forestry Action Programme. Activities should include setting up protected areas, surrounded by buffer and transition zones, conserving traditional habitats of indigenous communities and promoting their sustainable utilisation of forestry goods, planting of forests, greening human settlements, revegetating degraded areas and addressing social and ecological causes of destruction from shifting cultivation. Research on forest pollution, genetic resources, indigenous knowledge and forest inventories should be undertaken. Cooperation on transboundary air pollution and information exchange should be strengthened, activities of relevant intergovernmental organisations are supported.

The effective implementation of the UNCED Forest Principles are to be facilitated and supported, and ' .. on the basis of the implementation of these principles ... consider the need for and the feasibility of all kinds of appropriate internationally agreed arrangements to promote international cooperation on forest management, conservation and sustainable development of all types of forests ..'..

The sustainable production of **forestry goods and services**, including ecotourism and supply of genetic material should be promoted in the future. 'Social, economic and ecological values' of forests and 'efficient, rational and sustainable utilisation' for forest products should be recognised. A sustainable forestry production should promote the use of wood as energy sources, implement studies on forest utilisation, develop management guidelines, improve forest harvesting methods, including conversion and better use of forest products, residues and non-wood products to higher value end products. Wildlife management and comprehensive forest value accounting should be promoted, the ITTO Guidelines for Sustainable Management of Tropical Forests should be implemented. Accounting and assessment methods for the full value of forests should be established. Market surveys of forest products and services and trade opportunities should be provided. International trade of forest products should promote '... fair terms of trade, without resorting to unilateral restrictions and/or bans ..'..

**Assessment and systematic observations** of forests should increasingly be undertaken to deal with long-term issues and to analyse the impacts of programmes and projects. The situation and changes of forest resources, forest cover and land use should be assessed quantitatively and qualitatively, emphasising the role of national institutions and systems. The derived information should be disseminated and made available to planning and decision-making. Scientific effort should be directed to development of evaluation methodology, remote sensing, geographic information systems and others.

*The forest chapter, which forms a general and more coherent backdrop to the Forest Principles, was mainly agreed before Rio. The cross-reference to the Forest Principles was renegotiated at Rio, as was the delicate and non-committal wording pointing to the possibility of other 'appropriately agreed international arrangements' - a far cry from the hopes of developed countries for the launch of negotiations on a Forest Convention (see section 5.2).*

## CHAPTER 12: MANAGING FRAGILE ECOSYSTEMS: COMBATING DESERTIFICATION AND DROUGHT

Desertification affects deserts, arid, semi-arid and dry-subhumid areas, ie. one-quarter of the world's land surface. It can be related to climate, human activities and other factors. Taking appropriate action needs sufficient **knowledge** on desertification processes. Environmental information systems, systematic observation systems and networking and coordination should be established and strengthened. Data collection and monitoring systems should be approached in an integrated manner. Impact assessment and integrated research programmes and national institutions should be enhanced. International cooperation and local participation should be strengthened.

Preventive measures should be adopted with the overall aim to increase the vegetation cover of the land in danger of degradation, ie. through **soil**

**conservation, afforestation and reforestation**. Preventive measures for areas not yet or only slightly desertified should be undertaken with priority, but rehabilitative measures for the moderately to severely desertified areas should not be neglected. Activities on agroforestry should be community based, incentives for forestry investment should be introduced, reducing the pressure on woodfuel should be promoted. Measures should recognise indigenous and traditional knowledge and practices.

**Integrated development programmes** for agropastoral systems should be addressed to provide alternative livelihood systems and to eradicate poverty. It should be approached in a decentralised way through participation of local groups and strengthening of rural activities. Cottage production and business, rural banking systems and entrepreneurship should be promoted. Relevant information should be made available, international coordination and cooperation should be strengthened.

Because the functioning of natural ecosystems is important for socio-economic development, **comprehensive anti-desertification programmes** should be integrated into national development planning. Relevant institutions and authorities at all levels and its coordination and cooperation should be strengthened, strategic thinking and activities in planning and monitoring should be enhanced. The UN General Assembly is requested 'to establish ... an intergovernmental negotiating committee for the elaboration of an international convention to combat desertification, in those countries experiencing serious drought and/or desertification, particularly in Africa, with a view to finalizing such a convention by June 1994'. International cooperation on integrated desertification programmes should be strengthened and national coordination should be improved.

The recurring **drought events** need short-term activities and long-term strategies to 'reduce the vulnerability of production systems to drought'. Early warning systems should be established and its information dissemination ensured; arrangements on food contingency and short-term employment, including the provision of relevant budgets, should be adopted. Drought relief schemes should be developed and measures for environmental refugees established.

Partnership between local and national government, NGOs and land users on drought and desertification issues is needed. Popular involvement and **participation** particularly of women and indigenous communities is to be strengthened. Local management plans should be developed and measures should be introduced 'to secure user involvement and access to land resources'.

Through environmental education, the awareness of the population on desertification issues should be strengthened.

*After decades of ineffective measures to halt desertification, the outcry of African countries succeeded in winning support for their call for an international convention as the only way of drawing international attention to their plight. After furious debates in Rio, a final compromise of chairman Koh was accepted when the USA switched towards supporting a convention, leaving as the only major obstacle last minute objections from the EC, which eventually withdrew its position that a full UN convention was not appropriate for such a 'regional' environmental issue. A central African hope is for more financial support through an international convention.*

## CHAPTER 13: MANAGING FRAGILE ECOSYSTEMS: SUSTAINABLE MOUNTAIN DEVELOPMENT

Mountains provide a variety of ecological niches and of resources, but are under threat of deterioration. The lack of **knowledge** on mountain ecosystems needs to be addressed. Information should be generated through mountain surveys and monitoring on ecological and resource issues on climate and hydrology. Traditional practices and technologies should be investigated and developed, *inter alia* for protection of genetic resources. Data collection and information exchange on environment and development of mountains should be improved, relevant institutions should be strengthened. Conservation of ecologically-rich mountain regions and sites should be enhanced, by involving local communities. The focus is on interdisciplinary research, ecological knowledge and local practices. Generated information on sustainable development of mountains should be disseminated and made available through networking and clearing-houses. Conservation activities of local communities and their application of traditional environmentally sound technologies should be promoted. The economic base of mountain regions should be diversified and genetic resources preserved.

Deterioration of mountain ecosystems through deforestation, soil erosion and cultivation of marginal lands threatens the ecological balance and the livelihood of their, and adjacent, populations. 'By the year 2000, ... appropriate land-use planning and management ..'. is to be developed, ie. prevention and control of soil erosion and **integrated watershed development**. Participation of local people, particularly women and indigenous communities is to be enhanced. Alternative livelihood opportunities should be promoted, through tourism, small scale agro-industries etc. To protect species and ecosystems, threatened areas should be preserved. In disaster prone areas, measures to mitigate risks should be undertaken.

*A combination of mountain associations with the Swiss, Nepalese and other interested governments introduced this chapter which was readily adopted before Rio.*

## CHAPTER 14: PROMOTING SUSTAINABLE AGRICULTURE AND RURAL DEVELOPMENT

Increasing food demands in the future and environmental and socio-economic problems of agricultural production require new approaches, including **planning and integrated programmes with regard to food security and sustainable development**. Integrated programmes on sustainable agricultural development should be established by 1995 and operational multisectoral plans on agricultural development and food security by 1998; the institutional capacities in developing countries should be enhanced not later than 2005. Measures against fragmentation of agricultural land should be promoted and activities on food security should be strengthened, and UN and other bodies should, with governments, 'encourage .. a more open and non-discriminatory trading system and the avoidance of unjustifiable trade barriers'.

Sustainable agriculture and rural development relies on full **participation** of the rural population and strengthened public awareness. '... equitable access of rural people ... to land, water and forest resources and to technologies, financing ..'. is to be ensured, with particular attention to equal access of women. Decentralised decisionmaking is to be promoted, rural communities and their organisations should be strengthened.

To increase agricultural productivity, farming should encourage **diversification** of production systems. Employment creation, particularly for the poor should be promoted on-farm and off-farm; rural capabilities and infrastructure should be strengthened to allow self-development of farmers and rural communities.

To counteract the widespread degradation of land resources, **agricultural planning** should be improved at all levels. Particular attention should be given to local activities, systematic approaches and implementation of planning measures. Data on sustainable agriculture should increasingly be collected, its information should be made available through databases.

To strengthen the **conservation and rehabilitation** of land resources, causes of land degradation and inappropriate land use are to be removed, focusing on vulnerable and degraded areas. Land degradation surveys are to be established at national level by the year 2000. Both short-term urgent action and long-term strategies should be addressed; comprehensive programmes for land conservation and reclamation are needed, public participation should be strengthened.

**Plant genetic resources** are not yet preserved adequately. Their possible future agricultural value should be recognised; relevant institutions concerned of their conservation and sustainable use should be strengthened and institutional cooperation promoted. Programmes on both in situ on-farm and ex-situ conservation should be established not later than the year 2000. Multiplication and regeneration of collected plant species should be enhanced. Both conservation and research activities should be encouraged through ' ... fair and equitable sharing of benefits ... between the sources and users of plant genetic resources'.

**Animal genetic resources** are increasingly under threat. Local animal breeds with their specific adaptation and disease resistance should be preserved. A 10-year programme of action for the description of all breeds of livestock is needed; endangered animal species should be identified. Programmes to preserve breeds at risk should be established and measures for the survival and development of indigenous animal breeds undertaken.

To overcome the problems of conventional chemical pest control, **integrated pest management** should be promoted, it 'combines biological control, host plant resistance and appropriate farming practices' by reduced pesticide application. Integrated pest management should be made available to farmers; networks among research and practice should be established from 1998 or earlier. The use of pesticides should be monitored and the safe and appropriate application ensured through national policies. The International Code of Conduct on the Distribution and Use of Pesticides (FAO, 1989) should be implemented not later than 2000. Plant protection and animal health services should be provided from 2000 or earlier. Pesticide labelling should be improved and non-chemical ways of pest control promoted.

The **plant nutrient** depletion should return towards a balance, by adopting the integrated plant nutrition approach, ie. 'ensuring a sustainable supply of plant nutrients to increase future yields without harming the environment and soil productivity'. From the year 2000 or earlier, this approach should be established in all countries, the supply of fertilizers and plant nutrients should be improved and activities on soil productivity should be strengthened. National policies should address soil fertility maintenance, recycling of wastes and 'national accounting' of plant nutrients.

**Rural energy** policies should 'promote a mix of cost-effective fossil and renewable energy sources ..'., until the year 2000 rural communities should start 'a process of environmentally sound energy transition' away from unsustainable energy technologies. Particularly renewable energy sources and energy efficiency should be strengthened, the overall energy supply for rural needs should be increased.

Because of the depletion of the stratospheric ozone layer, the **UV radiation** on the Earth's surface is likely to increase. Effects on plant and animal life and mitigation strategies should be investigated, and in affected areas appropriate remedial measures should be supported.

*This exceptionally large chapter reflects growing recognition of and concern about the links between intensive agriculture and environmental degradation on one hand, and problems of hunger, oversupply, trade and price support on the other. It represents a significant advance in thinking about these issues in an integrated manner. Despite its scope, apart from references to finance and 'people under occupation', only the fair and equitable sharing in the context of plant genetic resources was still under discussion at Rio. The USA was concerned about implications for its biotechnology industry, but finally withdrew its opposition to this phrase.*

CHAPTER 15: CONSERVATION OF BIOLOGICAL DIVERSITY

The diversity of the world's species is continuously declining, mainly caused by human activities. In situ protection as well as ex situ conservation should be strengthened. The Convention on Biological Diversity is supported, an early entry into force and 'the widest possible participation' are promoted. '... national strategies for the conservation of biological diversity and the sustainable use of biological resources' should be developed and integrated into national development plans. Country studies and world assessments of biodiversity should be carried out, the cost and benefits of related activities should be analysed. '... fair and equitable sharing of benefits derived from research and development and use of biological and genetic resources, including biotechnology between sources of those resources and those who use them', should be adopted; the detailed rights of countries of origin are still to be defined and developed. Traditional knowledge and practices, particularly of indigenous communities and women, in the conservation and sustainable use of biological resources should be supported, benefits of the use of their methods should be shared with these communities. The contribution of biotechnology to biodiversity conservation and sustainable use should be investigated and further research on the importance of the biodiversity for the global ecosphere should be undertaken. International cooperation and technology transfer should be promoted. National efforts should address strategies of conservation and sustainable use and their integration into other policy areas. Environmental impact assessments of relevant projects and protected area systems should be established. Traditional knowledge and practices should be promoted.

*Several contentious paragraphs were left bracketed for final negotiations at Rio, pending completion of the Biodiversity Convention which was concluded after PrepCom IV. Issues such as sharing of benefits, technology transfer and national registration of biological resources were then adopted in this chapter using language of the Convention.*

## CHAPTER 16: ENVIRONMENTALLY SOUND MANAGEMENT OF BIOTECHNOLOGY

Biotechnology offers opportunities to contribute significantly to sustainable development in the future, but its environmentally sound management is to be ensured.

The need for increasing **food production** should be approached in a variety of ways: optimising the yield of crops and livestock by application of modern biotechnology and conventional methods, shifting to a higher nutritional values and reducing pre- and post-harvest losses; adopting integrated pest management, and, investigating symbiotic processes, particularly nitrogen fixation. Forestry research should focus on fast growing trees. Resistance to diseases and pests and preventive measures against diseases should be investigated. Integration of appropriate and traditional biotechnologies to modify plant and animal species and use of biotechnology to improve the yields of aquatic systems are to be promoted.

Degradation of the environment, malnutrition etc. raises much concern about increasing deterioration of **human health**, the following applications of biotechnology should be investigated: combatement of major communicable and non-communicable diseases through development of new vaccines, biological control agents against disease-transmitting vectors, new drugs, diagnostics and medical technologies. Research on general health, water related diseases, medical plants and improved delivery systems.

Appropriate use of biotechnology could deal with some of our **environmental problems**, eg. biomass recycling, waste water treatment and land rehabilitation. Applications in agriculture are proposed for bio-fertilizers, biological pest control agents and improved planting materials. Biotechnological applications should contribute to optimize industrial processes, ie. energy recovery, waste minimisation and higher yields of favoured products.

To ensure the **safety** of biotechnology, internationally agreed principles on risk assessment and management are to be developed. Existing safety procedures should be widely disseminated and improved. The principles should particularly address health and environmental issues, they should allow 'the widest possible public participation' and should 'take account of ethical considerations'. Biotechnological releases, international cooperation and exchange of information should be strengthened and the development of guidelines considered.

Development and **application** of biotechnologies should be promoted, particularly in developing countries, *inter alia* through facilitating their access, enhancing awareness of the public and decisionmakers, strengthening endogenous capacities and institutions and increasing dissemination of information. Traditional knowledge of indigenous communities should be recognised, benefits from the development of related biotechnologies should be shared with these people.

*This aims to foster internationally-agreed principles for the management of biotechnology and to promote its sustainable application. The chapter provides a more general framework than the specific measures in the Biodiversity Convention (see Chapter 7), and many paragraphs of this chapter were still under discussion in Rio. The USA was concerned about too much emphasis on safety of biotechnology, while the EC was primarily concerned about social, economic and environmental impacts of biotechnology applications. The Holy See successfully introduced amendments on reproductive health technologies. The wording on capacity-building was replaced by language from the technology transfer chapter. The final compromise recognised benefits for indigenous knowledge and practices and the need to develop safety procedures internationally.*

CHAPTER 17: PROTECTION OF THE OCEANS, ALL KINDS OF SEAS, INCLUDING ENCLOSED AND SEMI-ENCLOSED SEAS, AND COASTAL AREAS AND THE PROTECTION, RATIONAL USE AND DEVELOPMENT OF THEIR LIVING RESOURCES

The marine environment, ie. oceans, seas and coastal areas, is an important part of the global ecosphere. The basis for international regulation is given by the 1982 UN Convention on the Law of the Sea (UNCLOS),[3] further work of various levels on marine sustainable management and development is required. Activities of developing countries regarding the marine environment need additional financial resources and access to clean technologies.

The current, often degrading management of the **coastal environment** should be transformed to an 'integrated management and sustainable development of coastal areas and the marine environment under their national jurisdiction', ie. the exclusive economic zone (EEZ). Integrated policies should adopt appropriate land and water use and siting policies and should develop sectoral programmes, eg. on tourism, fishery and human settlements. In project planning, environmental impact assessments should be undertaken and the precautionary approach applied. The establishment of national and local coordinating mechanisms for integrated management and sustainable development of the coastal environment should be considered.

Policy measures should *inter alia* integrate **marine environmental protection** into overall development policies and adopt economic incentives. A variety of contaminants causes marine pollution, the major sources are land-based activities. It is aimed 'to prevent, reduce and control degradation of the marine environment so as to maintain and improve its life-support and productive capacities'. To reduce land-based emission, enhanced sewage treatment should be addressed with priority, the Montreal Guidelines[4] should be strengthened, regional agreements should be initiated and improved. To this end an intergovernmental meeting should be convened, organised by the

---

[3] UNCLOS is nine ratifications away from formal entry into force, but most states accept it as representing customary international law outside of its deep seabed mining provisions, which were the central source of dispute and the main reason for the continuing US refusal to sign.
[4] *Guidelines for the Protection of the Marine Environment against Pollution from Land-Based Sources*, Montreal, 1985.

UNEP Governing Council. The main sources of sea-based marine pollution are emissions from shipping and dumping, reduction measures should be taken here and also for oil and gas platforms and ports.

The over-utilisation of **marine living resources** of the high seas and under national jurisdiction is of concern. These resources should increasingly be managed in a sustainable manner and be conserved, ie. protection of species and habitats, improved fishing activities and use as a source of human nutrients. In accordance with the Law of the Sea, sustainable management of fisheries populations, aqua- and mari-culture should be implemented. The special needs of artisanal fisheries should be addressed, the interests of local communities and their traditional knowledge should be taken into account. States should control appropriate activities of vessels flying their flags and prohibit destructive fishing practices. A conference on straddling and highly migratory fish stocks should be convened by recognising provisions of the Law of the Sea and drawing on FAO work. The work of the International Whaling Commission is recognised. Data collection and information exchange on marine living resources should be enhanced. International and regional cooperation on improved seafood availability, including minimising waste and by-catch, should be upgraded particularly for developing countries. Beyond fishery, the ecological function of coral reefs and other habitats should be recognised.

The marine environment is an important system within the global ecosphere and is vulnerable to **climate change**. Scientific research, systematic observation and its information exchange should be promoted, aiming to improve forecast methods. Impact research of increased UV radiation should be enhanced. The importance of Antarctica for global environmental research is recognised. Efforts to establish human resources in marine sciences, national oceanographic commissions and endogenous research capabilities should be undertaken.

**Cooperation and coordination** should be based on integrated and multisectoral approaches, institutional arrangements should be strengthened, intergovernmental reviews on marine issues of environment and development promoted and effective coordination should be established within the UN system, eg. regular consultations within the General Assembly, and between other organisations. Regional and sub-regional cooperation, eg. Regional Seas Programmes of UNEP, should be strengthened.

**Small island states** are particularly vulnerable to global environmental changes, their social and economic development options are particularly disadvantaged. Programmes are to be implemented to support their sustainable development and to counteract the implications of likely environmental changes in the future. Development and utilisation of appropriate technologies for their local requirements should be promoted. A global conference and periodic meetings on sustainable development of small island developing states should be convened.

*This is the longest and one of the most complex chapters of Agenda 21. Intense negotiations throughout PrepComs III and IV reached an uneasy compromise on the conservation of whales and other cetaceans and a number of other contentious issues, excepting that of straddling and migratory fish stocks. On this subject the USA (which had made major inputs to the chapter) finally brokered a compromise between Canada and the EC in Rio, resulting in the call for an intergovernmental conference to promote effective implementation of the Law of the Sea provisions on this subject taking account of UNCLOS provisions and FAO studies.*

## CHAPTER 18: PROTECTION OF THE QUALITY AND SUPPLY OF FRESHWATER RESOURCES: APPLICATION OF INTEGRATED APPROACHES TO THE DEVELOPMENT, MANAGEMENT AND USE OF WATER RESOURCES

Freshwater is an important part of the global environment. While water is needed for various human activities, its scarcity, destruction and pollution becomes obvious in many regions.

The widespread demands for agricultural, industrial and domestic purposes require **integrated water management**, ie. 'water as an integral part of the ecosystem, a natural resource and a social and economic good ..'.. National action plans, institutions and legal arrangements as well as efficiency programmes should be established by the year 2000, sub-sectoral targets of all freshwater programme areas should be achieved by 2025; the implementation in developing countries requires additional funding. A variety of measures for integrated water management were proposed, including flood and drought management, water conservation and rational water use, integrated quantity and quality management, demand management, decentralisation of water management and support to water-user groups.

To obtain more information on water quality and quantity and its possible use, **water resources assessments** should be undertaken. Activities of the Mar del Plata Action Plan[5] are recognised, and assessments of quality and quantity, supply and demand of water resources should be strengthened. Water assessment technology and financial resources should be provided to all countries, relevant human resources and an institutional framework should be developed, assessment information should be provided to relevant decisionmaking processes. Feasibility studies of assessment services should be undertaken by the year 2000. Data collection systems and data dissemination should be strengthened, to allow appropriate water planning decisions.

Freshwater, 'a unitary resource', should be **protected** in an integrated and preventive manner. Human needs and environmental considerations should be balanced. The integration of water-quality elements into water resource management needs aquatic ecosystems preservation, public health protection and human resources development. A variety of specific activities at national level are proposed: addressing protection and conservation of water resources, prevention and control of water pollution, protection of aquatic ecosystems and of groundwater and monitoring of water resources. Scientific research centres and multidisciplinary research programmes, particularly working on problems of developing countries, should be developed. Local human resources should be strengthened and water protection capacities improved.

Great concern about diseases and deaths caused by contamination of **drinking water** needs to be addressed urgently. Regarding the New Delhi Statement, 'the need to provide, on a sustainable basis, access to safe water in sufficient quantities and proper sanitation for all, emphasising the "some for all rather than more for some approach"' is recognised. Management of water resources and wastes should be integrated; institutions should adopt this integrated approach, activities should be community driven and women should fully participate, appropriate technologies and sound financial practices should be applied. Universal access to water supply should be provided by 2025; activities should focus on low-cost services but the annual financial resources still need to be doubled. Specific activities cover environment and health

---

[5] In 1981, the International Drinking Water Supply and Sanitation Decade was launched, as a result of the Mar del Plata Action Plan adopted by the United Nations Water Conference in 1977. *Report of the United Nations Water Conference, Mar del Plata, 14-25 March 1977*, United Nations, No. E.77.II.A.12.

issues, people and institutions, national and community management, and awareness creation and public information and participation. Technological means should focus on support for developing countries, ie. low-cost systems, traditional practices and institutional assistance.

Because of the rapidly growing population in cities, **urban water resources** are to be developed rapidly. By the year 2000, everybody in cities should have access to 40l/day/capita of safe water, water sanitation and waste management and disposal should be provided to 75 % of the urban population and sewage discharge standards should be established. Urban water resources should be protected from depletion, pollution and degradation and should be shared equally and used efficiently. Local institutions should be strengthened, and sanitary services particularly for the urban poor should be improved.

In rural areas, water resources are needed for the human population and for food production, ie. irrigation, livestock, fishery and agro-forestry. Environmentally sound **rural water management** should focus on the finite nature of water resources, on its present and future role for meeting basic needs and on participation of local communities, by fully involving women. It should be addressed comprehensively within a framework of related issues, ie. human health, food production, disaster mitigation and nature conservation. The work of the FAO's International Action Programme on Water and Sustainable Agricultural Development is recognised, particularly on irrigation development. The improvement of existing irrigation schemes should be given priority before constructing new ones. Various activities cover the following areas: water-supply and sanitation for the unserved rural poor; water use efficiency; water logging, salinity control and drainage; water-quality management; water resources development programmes; scarce water resources management; water supply for livestock; inland fisheries; aquaculture development. Scientific expertise should focus on water monitoring, agricultural water inventories, fish production potentials and dissemination of data.

**Climate change** can affect quality and quantity of freshwater resources substantially. Research efforts should investigate the impact of climate change on water systems particularly in areas prone to flood and drought. National policy measures should be studied. Techniques and methodologies of climate change impact assessment, hydrologic monitoring, brackish-water use in agriculture and other issues should be investigated. Further research of IPCC, the International Geosphere-Biosphere Programme (IGBP) etc., particularly on response strategies, should be strengthened.

*Another very large chapter, this drew heavily upon the work of the Dublin Conference on Water and the Environment.[6] The approach of the freshwater chapter was similar to that of the conference report, but France and the UK did not succeed in their efforts to include specific reference or endorsement of the Dublin Conference.*

## CHAPTER 19: ENVIRONMENTALLY SOUND MANAGEMENT OF TOXIC CHEMICALS INCLUDING PREVENTION OF ILLEGAL INTERNATIONAL TRAFFIC IN TOXIC AND DANGEROUS PRODUCTS

Risks associated with the handling and use of chemicals require their assessment and regulation 'to ensure the environmentally sound management of toxic chemicals'. Only a limited number of the about 100,000 commercial chemical substances are yet assessed for their risks to human health and the environment, much effort on **international risk assessment** of chemicals is still to be undertaken, major pollutants should be assessed by the year 2000. Guidelines should set acceptable human and environmental exposure limits. Existing programmes on chemical risk assessment, eg. the International Programme on Chemical Safety (IPCS),[7] should be expanded. Collaboration among governments, industry, academia and NGOs is to be strengthened. Data should be provided by the industry and/or generated by the existing international programmes. A system of priority setting for the assessment of chemicals should be established. Research on alternatives to toxic chemicals and on methods to replace animal testing should be strengthened.

To make handling and use of chemicals safer globally, a harmonised hazard **classification and labelling system** should be established by the year 2000. Material safety data sheets and easily understandable symbols should be developed.

---

[6] Water Supply and Sanitation Collaborative Council, *International Conference on Water and the Environment: Development Issues for the 21st century*, 26-31 January 1992, Dublin: The Dublin statement and Report of the Conference, (Geneva, 1992). This was a UN-sponsored conference of experts, not governments, with agreement reached by vote rather than consensus; hence formal references to it were rejected in Agenda 21 negotiations.

[7] Jointly organised by UNEP, ILO and WHO in 1980, 'to assess the risks that specific chemicals pose to human health and the environment' UNEP, *Saving Our Planet: Challenges and Hopes, The State of the Environment 1972-1992*, UNEP, Nairobi, 1992.

The **exchange of information** on chemical safety, use and emissions should be strengthened. Prior Informed Consent (PIC) procedures should be adopted, as introduced in the London Guidelines[8] and the FAO international pesticide code of conduct.[9]

**Risk reduction programmes** aim to eliminate unacceptable risks and to substitute toxic chemicals by less harmful substances. The entire life cycle of products should be analysed. Governments should *inter alia* adopt producer liability principles, preventive measures against accidents and emergency responses procedures. Industry should establish a code of principles on chemical trade, adopt a 'responsible care' approach and should consider community-right-to-know programmes. International cooperation on risk reduction should be strengthened.

International measures for chemical safety rely on adequate **national capacities and capabilities**, ie. legislation, effective implementation and enforcement. National systems for environmentally sound management of chemicals should be established by the year 2000. Institutional mechanisms are to be established and adequate coordination of all relevant parties is to be achieved. Preparedness for accidents should be ensured, including emergency response centres and emergency plans. International cooperation should support the effort of developing countries on chemical safety rules. International principles for accident prevention should be promoted.

**Transboundary movement** of toxic products is of international concern. Measures for detection and prevention of illegal international traffic should be undertaken, national capacities including regulatory measures and enforcement programmes are to be strengthened. Developing countries are to be assisted in their effort. National alert systems, regional monitoring and assessment and arrangements for international exchange of information on the movement of toxic products should be established.

*The central concerns of this chapter are the problems posed by the lack of adequate information for assessing the risks posed by toxic chemicals, and the problems of preventing illegal traffic in them. Difficult negotiations in the PrepComs led to a chapter that was accepted without difficulty at Rio.*

---

[8] London Guidelines for the Exchange of Information, UNEP Governing Council, 1989.
[9] International Code of Conduct on the Distribution and Use of Pesticides, FAO, 1989.

...s were left to be negotiated in Rio. The G-77 countries opposed ...rgets without agreement on additional funding and concessional ...ropriate technologies.

## ...R 22: SAFE AND ENVIRONMENTALLY SOUND ...EMENT OF RADIOACTIVE WASTES

...ctive wastes, in increasing amounts generated by nuclear energy ...sses and other nuclear applications, should be managed by reducing its ...act on human health and the environment. 'The safe and environmentally ...nd management of radioactive wastes' should focus on minimising the ...eneration of wastes in the first place, reducing the impact of the generated ...wastes by making storage, transportation and processing safer and implementing its safe disposal. Planning methods, including environmental impact assessment, should be strengthened; the development of safety standards and guidelines by the IAEA should be supported. Specific measures on international cooperation are proposed to strengthen and implement international agreements and conventions, including implementing the Code of Practice on the Transboundary Movements of Radioactive Waste, to introduce a ban on dumping of low-level radioactive wastes in the sea under the London Dumping Convention,[12] and to abandon, as appropriate, the storage and disposal of radioactive wastes near the sea. Further research on radioactive waste management technologies and on impact assessment should be undertaken.

*This chapter sparked difficult debates between countries with differing approaches to radioactive waste management. The USA appeared particularly concerned about allowing international control of its activities. Compromise language on this and concerning storage or disposal near the marine environment was left to Rio.*

## 9.4 Section III: Strengthening the role of major groups

The preamble to Section III states that the 'global partnership for sustainable development' needs a broad **participation of all groups and organisations**

[12] Convention on the Prevention of Marine Pollution by Dumping of Wastes and Other Matter, London, 1972.

---

## CHAPTER 20: ENVIRONMENTALLY SOUND MANAGEMENT OF HAZARDOUS WASTES INCLUDING PREVENTION OF ILLEGAL INTERNATIONAL TRAFFIC IN HAZARDOUS WASTES

Hazardous wastes are produced in increasing amounts, its management and disposal needs appropriate national institutions and international cooperation. Transboundary movements are of increasing international concern, particularly its illegal traffic. The global Basel Convention[10] and African Bamako Convention[11] should be ratified and implemented.

The most environmentally sound way to deal with hazardous wastes is to **prevent** or at least to **minimise** its generation. National strategies should aim to stabilise the generation of hazardous wastes and to reduce its hazardous characteristics as an intermediate stage and to reduce the amount in a long-term programme. Governments should promote recovery of materials, cleaner production methods and technology assessments. They should establish domestic hazardous waste treatment and disposal facilities and strengthen the transfer of relevant technologies to developing countries. Industry should deal with hazardous wastes at the source of generation and should establish environmental management systems. Information on cleaner production should be collected and disseminated internationally.

Many problems of hazardous waste and its transboundary movement can be related to the lack of **institutional capacities**. Governments should adopt legislation on environmentally sound management of hazardous wastes and establish comprehensive research programmes. Awareness of the public and of workers should be strengthened on hazardous waste issues through education and training programmes. Endogenous capacities in developing countries should be improved. Assessments and inventories on human exposure and health risks should be promoted.

**International cooperation** on hazardous waste management should be strengthened, including control of transboundary movement. Export to countries which do not have appropriate treatment or disposal facilities should be prohibited. Transboundary movement for recycling and recovery should be controlled. Criteria and guidelines for hazardous waste management should be harmonised and strengthened internationally.

[10] Basel Convention on the Control of Transboundary Movements of Hazardous Wastes and their Disposal, 22 March 1989, Basel, Switzerland.
[11] Bamako Convention on the Ban on the Import into Africa and the Control of Transboundary Movement of Hazardous Wastes within Africa, OAU, Bamako, Mali, 1991.

Illegal **transboundary movement** of hazardous wastes should be prevented, effective monitoring and appropriate penalties are required. Institutions should be strengthened to detect and halt the illegal import of hazardous wastes, assistance should be given particularly to developing countries on issues of illegal traffic. Regulatory measures should be adopted to prevent illegal import and export of hazardous wastes, detection of violations should be strengthened. Exchange of relevant information, networks and alert systems should be promoted.

*A total ban on an exports of hazardous wastes to developing countries was not adopted. Instead language from the Basel Convention was introduced. The G77 countries would not agree that financial resources should be provided to economies in transition. References to military establishments were questioned by the USA, but compromise language was found to recognise them as an important source of waste and consequently on the need for them to 'conform to their nationally applicable environmental norms in the treatment and disposal of hazardous waste'.*

## CHAPTER 21: ENVIRONMENTALLY SOUND MANAGEMENT OF SOLID WASTES AND SEWAGE-RELATED ISSUES

The environmentally sound management of solid wastes is closely related to other issues: freshwater, human settlements, human health and consumption patterns. The hierarchy of integrated solid waste management patterns addresses as its first objective their minimisation, second, reuse and recycling, and finally, disposal and treatment including the extension of service coverage. In practice, strategies should adopt a comprehensive framework by recognising local conditions. Preventive waste management emphasises changing lifestyles and patterns of consumption and production.

Governments should adopt the following **waste minimisation** policies: by the year 2000, all countries should have developed capacities for monitoring waste and implementing waste minimisation strategies, and developed countries in particular should address policies dealing with specific waste problems, eg. packaging materials, by the year 2000. Procedures and methods of waste assessment and monitoring should be developed; relevant institutional capacities should be strengthened. The instruments utilised, their effectiveness and impacts of the waste minimisation policies should be reviewed periodically

and relevant information disseminated. N̄ should become a principle objective o᷄ integrated into national develoᵖ technological developments should be̩ countries facilitated.

Waste **reuse and recycling** capabilitie᷄ national recycling programmes should be adoᵖ by 2000 and in developing countries by 2010. Recyᷓ are to be strengthened, pilot projects should be promoᷛ on techniques and methods should be disseminated᷄ guidelines and provide incentives to increase recycling, eg᷄ recycled materials. Measures should be reviewed to improve ᵘ Research efforts should focus on pilot programmes, improving developing innovative techniques. The transfer of recycling teᵉ should be facilitated.

An increasing proportion of generated wastes should be **treated** **disposed** of safely. In industrialised countries, standards should be improveᵈ while in developing countries some kind of treatment and disposal should be initiated. By the year 2000, quality criteria and standards as well as monitoring and surveillance capacities should be established. In the case of sewage, waste waters and solid wastes, 50% should be treated and disposed according quality guidelines by 1995 in industrialised countries and by 2005 in developing countries. For all wastes, this should be achieved by 2025. Programmes on waste-related pollution should be undertaken, through strengthening of national capacities, collection and dissemination of relevant information and by implementing environmentally sound and efficient measures to treat and dispose wastes close to its place of source. Pollution standards should be set and monitoring programmes established.

The extent of **waste service coverage** in urban areas - particularly of developing countries - as yet is very unsatisfactory. Many deaths are caused by waste-related diseases. By 2000, a waste collection service should be provided and by 2025 adequate waste services for all urban populations should be provided. Full urban waste service coverage should be maintained and rural sanitation coverage provided by 2025. To extend services, particular emphasis should be given to serving the needs of the poor. Service should be provided under the polluter-pays principle, but financing mechanisms for deprived areas are to be established.

in decisionmaking. Consequently, 'Individuals, groups and organisations should have access to information relevant to environment and development ..'.. The 10 individual chapters which form this section (nos 23-32)[13] have many themes in common and are here considered together.

The active involvement of **women** in decisionmaking is needed. International agreements and strategies to eliminate discrimination against women and for the advancement of women are supported. The proportion of women in high-profile jobs related to sustainable development should be increased. Women's NGOs should be strengthened and strategies 'to eliminate ... obstacles to women's full participation in sustainable development and in public life' should be developed. By 1995, assessment mechanisms should be established, how women could participate in sustainable development activities and how they could be affected and could benefit. A variety of more specific measures were outlined, including equitable access to resources, proper valuation of the role and activities of women in societies, improved education for girls and women, equal employment opportunities and equitable remuneration, education and awareness activities to eliminate discrimination and negative images against women. Review of progress should be reported to the 1995 world conference on women, states should review the Convention on the Elimination of All Forms of Discrimination against Women (UN, 18 December, 1979) by the year 2000.

**Children and youth** should participate in decisionmaking processes because their futures will be shaped by today's policies. By the year 1993, **youth** should be consulted on environmental policies; a 'dialogue between the youth community and government' should be promoted. 'Access of all youth to all types of education, where appropriate,' should be ensured and secondary education for more than 50 % of both sexes by the year 2000 should be achieved. Unemployment of young people should be reduced and alternative employment strategies should be developed. Youth representation in UN processes and in delegations of international meetings should be established. Further measures include combatement of human rights abuses, awareness

---

[13] The full chapter titles are: 23: Preamble to Section III; 24: Global action for women towards sustainable and equitable development; 25: Children and youth in sustainable development; 26: Recognising and strengthening the role of indigenous people and their communities; 27: Strengthening the role of non-governmental organisations: partners for sustainable development; 28: Local authorities' initiatives in support of Agenda 21; 29: Strengthening the role of workers and their trade unions; 30: Strengthening the role of business and industry; 31: Scientific and technological community; 32: Strengthening the role of farmers.

programmes developed by youth on youth issues and the review of international youth programmes.

**Children** suffer heavily from environmental deterioration and are therefore particularly concerned about environmental issues. Their concerns should be taken into account in sustainable development policies. The Convention on the Rights of the Child[14] should be ratified and implemented, recommendations of the 1990 World Summit for Children should be adopted. Programmes for children on health, nutrition, education, literacy and poverty alleviation should be implemented for the 1990s. Primary environmental care should be promoted and children's education improved. UNICEF should continue to coordinate children's activities internationally.

'**Indigenous people and their communities** have a historical relationship with their lands', their traditional sustainable management conserves their environment. The International Labour Organisation (ILO) Indigenous and Tribal Peoples Convention (No. 169), the draft universal declaration on indigenous rights, and the International Year for the World's Indigenous People (1993) are supported. Indigenous people should be consulted and actively participate in the resource management and development of their areas and should be involved in sustainable development strategies for their areas, regional issues should be adopted in a cooperative manner. Their communities should be empowered, by *inter alia* protection of their lands, arranging the resolution of disputes, recognising their dependency structures, practices and values, and enhancing capacity-building with international assistance. States are encouraged to ratify and apply the relevant conventions and to protect and preserve their intellectual property and their practices. International organisations should adopt procedures to support indigenous communities and to coordinate related issues and should assist capacity-building programmes. Research and education should focus on improving the understanding of indigenous knowledge and practices and should enhance a more efficient management.

'**Non-governmental organisations** (NGOs) play a vital role in the shaping and implementation of participatory democracy'. They should become partners in the implementation of Agenda 21, ie. to promote the participation, review and evaluation of NGOs for the implementation of Agenda 21 and to recognise these activities in the UN reporting system. Their 'experience, expertise and capacity' should be recognised. International organisations, governments and NGOs should communicate and cooperate in the 'fullest possible' way;

---

[14] UNGA resolution 44/25, 20 November 1989.

nationally, a dialogue between all governments and NGOs including their networks should be established by 1995. The procedures and mechanisms for NGO involvement in decisionmaking should be reviewed; on national and international levels, NGOs should be allowed to participate in reviews of Agenda 21 implementation and their assessments should be taken into account in implementation measures of Agenda 21. The UN system and international organisations should address appropriate support mechanisms and access to information for NGOs, should enhance the procedures for opportunities of NGOs to contribute to policies of the UN and should draw on expertise of NGOs in its decisionmaking. A dialogue between national governments and NGOs as well as local authorities and local groups should be established. Governments should strengthen the role of NGOs in education and public awareness.

**Local authorities** are important in shaping environmental infrastructures, planning and policies because their governance is 'closest to the people'. Local authorities have a vital role in achieving the objectives of Agenda 21. They should consult their citizens, local organisations and private enterprises and should build a consensus on a 'local Agenda 21' by 1996. Consultation, cooperation and coordination among local authorities should be established or enhanced on an international level by 1993-94. Women and youth in particular should participate in the implementation of Agenda 21 and the awareness of households and citizens should be enhanced. A partnership of local authorities should be strengthened through international associations of cities and local authorities and through international organisations working in that field. Measures for supporting local authorities on their infrastructural and environmental management should be established, in particular information collection of international organisations on local strategies and consultations on international support and on sectoral activities.

**Workers and trade unions** should be actively involved in sustainable development activities. Their main concern is 'poverty alleviation and full and sustainable employment, which contribute to safe, clean and healthy environments ..'.. Tripartite collaboration between governments, trade unions and employers' organisations should be established, particularly on the implementation of Agenda 21. ILO conventions on workers' freedom of association and on the right to organise should be ratified and implemented. Environmental policies should be jointly developed by workers' and employers' organisations. Workers and trade unions should have access to relevant information. Education, training and retraining programmes, particularly on the working environment, should be strengthened. Other trade union activities should focus on participation in sustainable development activities of local communities and of regional and international organisations.

**Business and industry**, including transnational corporations, 'play a crucial role in the social and economic development of a country', they 'provide major trading, employment and livelihood opportunities', they 'can play a major role in reducing impacts on resource use and the environment' and should be encouraged 'to operate responsibly and efficiently and to implement longer-term policies'. Their participation in the implementation of Agenda 21 is important. Their environmental management could include preventive strategies, cleaner production, waste minimisation etc.

To achieve **cleaner production**, resources should be used more efficiently, including recycling and minimisation of waste. Governments should encourage internalisation of environmental costs and use economic incentives and regulation in an appropriate mix. Voluntary initiatives of the business community are encouraged, in particular the ICC Business Charter on Sustainable Development (see section 4.6) and the chemical industry's Responsible Care initiative. Companies are encouraged to report their environmental record and resource use and to increase their awareness and responsibility on environmental issues; databases and information systems on cleaner production should be strengthened. Cooperation on cleaner production technology and expertise within the industrial community should be promoted. Business organisations should cooperate with trade unions on sustainable development strategies.

**Responsible entrepreneurship** could significantly improve health and environment significantly. Natural resource management should be improved through implementation of the concept of stewardship; companies should adopt sustainable development strategies. A variety of specific measures are proposed, including training on environmental management of enterprises, partnership schemes between large and small businesses, national business councils for sustainable development, self-regulation and responsible and ethical management as well as worldwide corporate policies on sustainable development.

The **scientific and technological community** should 'make a more open and effective contribution to decision-making processes concerning environment and development'. A full partnership between scientific and technological community and the public should be developed. Interdisciplinary research should be strengthened, ethical principles and codes of practice should be implemented.

**Decisionmaking processes** should become more open and should allow the **interaction** with the scientific and technological community. Scientific and technological inputs are important for national sustainable development strategies, regional cooperation and international agreement formulation; efforts of the UN system on sustainable development policies should be strengthened by scientific expertise. 'Intergovernmental panels on development and environmental issues should be organized'. The general public and the scientific and technological community should increasingly exchange their ideas. Scientific research on environment and development should be published, disseminated and made available to decisionmakers and the public. During scientific consultations, 'various strands of public opinion [should be] represented'.

Scientists and technologists should be aware of their responsibilities for sustainable development and 'ethical awareness in environmental and developmental decision-making' should be increased. **Codes of practice and guidelines** for science and technology on environmentally sound and sustainable development should be developed, adopted and incorporated into legal material. Work on environmental and developmental ethics should be strengthened including a 'common value framework between the public and scientific communities,' and further education and training.

Strategies for sustainable agriculture, rural development and management of fragile ecosystems need to be centred on the people most involved, the **farmers,** here understood as rural people mainly working in farming, fishing and forestry. To adopt sustainable farming strategies, the decentralisation of decisionmaking processes should be encouraged. 'A policy framework ... for sustainable and efficient farming practices' should be developed and programmes on related areas should be adopted. The participation of farmers and their organisations should be ensured. Access to land for women and vulnerable groups should be improved. Organisations of farmers should be formed and strengthened. Economic incentives should encourage farmers to use resources efficiently and to adopt self-sufficient technologies. Farmers' organisations should be encouraged to exchange experience through networking and to contribute to agro-ecological and location-specific farming research.

*The section on groups and organisations reflects the strengthened role of NGOs in the UN system and in decisionmaking processes overall. The enhanced access to information and the ability to submit reports to the Sustainable Development Commission could be the most important improvement of the NGOs working base. These chapters were surprisingly adopted without much problem (possibly because chairman Koh left discussion to the very end of the final PrepCom when delegates were tired). The industrialised countries, particularly the USA, were keen in supporting the enhanced role of NGOs, while some G-77 countries were cautious, particularly where the governmental obligations to consult NGOs were proposed.*

## 9.5 Section IV: Means of implementation

CHAPTER 33: FINANCIAL RESOURCES AND MECHANISMS

The implementation of Agenda 21 in national policies requires 'substantial new and additional financial resources', their provision should be 'both adequate and predictable'. Financial resources on grant or concessional terms should be provided 'according to sound and equitable criteria and indicators' and should match the 'progressive implementation' of sustainable policies. The financial mechanisms addressed comprise bilateral ODA, replenishment of International Development Association (IDA) funds for soft loans and other multilateral ODA, the GEF, various forms of debt relief, and a range of other possible innovative sources.

The **ODA** statements reflect several groups of donor countries, those which have affirmed to reach the 'accepted United Nations target of 0.7 % of GNP for ODA', 'reaffirm their commitments ... and ... [if] not yet achieved ... agree ... to reach that target as soon as possible ..'., including some countries by the year 2000. 'Those countries which have already reached the target [should] continue to contribute to the common effort' of additional funding. Developed countries which have not committed themselves to the 0.7 % target (primarily the USA) 'agree to make their best efforts to increase their level of ODA'. Economies in transition and other countries 'may voluntarily augment the contributions of the developed countries'.

To 'maximise the availability of new and additional resources' and to 'use all available funding sources and mechanisms' for the implementation of Agenda 21 and other UNCED agreements, the following measures should be adopted:

- **IDA** replenishment should give special consideration to the statement by the President of the World Bank at UNCED (which called for an 'Earth

Increment' on soft loans) 'to help the poorest countries meet their ... objectives ... in Agenda 21';

- regional and sub-regional development banks and funds should be strengthened;
- the **GEF** 'should cover the agreed incremental costs of relevant activities under Agenda 21', ie. with global environmental benefits. It should be restructured *inter alia* for a 'universal participation' and 'transparent and democratic governance', with 'a balanced and equitable representation of the interests of developing countries' and 'due weight to the funding efforts of donor countries'. Financial resources should be made available 'under mutually agreed criteria without introducing new forms of conditionality'.

The role of **multilateral institutions**, UN bodies (particularly UNDP, UNEP), specialized agencies and bilateral assistance programmes should be strengthened.

**Debt** problems of the low- and middle-income countries should be solved 'durably', the Paris Club agreement of December 1991 'to provide debt relief for the poorest heavily indebted countries pursuing structural adjustment' should be implemented 'promptly'. Debt problems and relief measures should be kept under review.

Further activities should mobilise private funding, investment and innovative financing, including debt swaps, economic and fiscal incentives and reallocation of military funds. The financial measures, their progress and adequacy, are to be reviewed and monitored regularly by the CSD; and 'systematically combined [with] the monitoring of the implementation of Agenda 21'.

*Developing countries considered financial measures as the key issue for implementing Agenda 21. Negotiations were concluded in Rio at Ministerial level and went on to the very end. Compromise language was fought bitterly between North and South. The G-77 countries demanded that the UN goal for ODA of 0.7% of GNP from developed countries be reached by the year 2000. The USA reiterated that it had never accepted the goal, many other developed countries refused a timetable; the EC was divided with the UK and Germany the main opponents to the deadline. The administration of funds for Agenda 21 was another very contentious area. The compromise kept the GEF as major funding body, but called for its restructuring, ie. a transparent and accountable GEF reflecting some of the G-77 criticisms. Other contentious issues on which compromise was reached at Rio included conditionality of funding, statements on IDA replenishment (specific reference to an 'Earth Increment' was rejected) and debt relief (see also Appendix 1).*

## CHAPTER 34: TRANSFER OF ENVIRONMENTALLY SOUND TECHNOLOGY, COOPERATION AND CAPACITY-BUILDING

Environmentally sound technologies, including expertise, and related issues should be made available to developing countries. Developing countries should have access to relevant information on technological choices, thus international information exchange systems and clearing houses should be developed. Access to and transfer of environmentally sound technology should be promoted 'on favourable terms, including on concessional and preferential terms, as mutually agreed, taking into account the need to protect intellectual property rights as well as the special needs of developing countries for the implementation of Agenda 21'.

Specific measures should include policies and programmes to encourage public and private technology transfer and regulatory measures, including subsidies and tax policies, and appropriate mechanisms for improved access to and transfer of relevant technologies. National capacities, particularly in developing countries, should be built to develop and manage environmentally sound technologies, including human resource development and strengthening of research and development capacities.

The development of indigenous technology and technology assessment should be promoted, 'a collaborative network of research centres' should be established and 'programmes of cooperation and assistance' should be strengthened. The importance of technology transfer through business and commerce is recognised while on the one hand the availability to developing countries is of concern, on the other 'fair incentives to innovators' should be provided; here the role of patent and property rights should be examined. Long-term partnerships between holders and users of environmentally sound technologies, and between companies in developed and developing countries as well as joint ventures should be promoted.

*To improve the internal capabilities for sustainable development in developing countries, the availability of environmentally sound technologies is crucial. To many developing countries, these issues were second in importance only to the financial issues of the previous chapter, and many key parts of the chapter were only resolved late in the negotiations at Rio. The major disputes between the*

*USA especially and the G77 countries were on terms of transfer, the role of international business and the abuse of intellectual property rights.*

CHAPTER 35: SCIENCE FOR SUSTAINABLE DEVELOPMENT

Scientific knowledge of the Earth system should be improved. Scientific research should support the search for appropriate strategies for sustainable development, but 'lack of ... understanding should not be an excuse for postponing actions ..'.

The **scientific base** should be widened to meet the needs of environmental and developmental management. Relevant institutions and international cooperation should be strengthened. There is a need to improve the communication between science, politics and public, and the cooperation between scientists and public participation in decisionmaking. Indigenous knowledge should be included in scientific analysis; methodologies and tools should be developed, including environmental policy formulation, economic approaches and quality of life indicators.

The natural environment and changes caused by human beings are interlinked, thus our **scientific understanding** should be enhanced. Research programmes should investigate the biogeochemical cycles and ecological and geophysical systems and their interactions, including monitoring and observation systems and networking. The influence of human activities on the Earth's system should be assessed. The integration of a variety of disciplines should be promoted for research on 'the impacts of economic and social behaviour on the environment and of environmental degradation on local and global economies', including global change response strategies.

Further development towards long-term **scientific assessments** for present and future situations is needed. A standard methodology should be developed. Audits on environmental and developmental issues were proposed for every five years. Gathering-systems on a wide range of data should be coordinated. This should allow the development of policy strategies, the assessments should be made publicly available.

**Scientific capacities** on environment and development related issues should be promoted, particularly in developing countries. The scientific infrastructure should be strengthened, particularly in developing countries aiming to reduce the 'brain drain'. Scientific and technological databases and information networks should be developed, access to relevant information should be ensured, including for the public. Institutional partnerships and multidisciplinary activities, including on policy strategies, should be promoted.

*This chapter, which overlaps substantially with the special groups chapter on scientists, was easily completed at PrepCom IV. Neither chapter mentions the Secretary-General's specific proposals for an 'Earth Council' of independent experts, but clearly support the need for independent advisory groups in general.*


CHAPTER 36: PROMOTING EDUCATION, PUBLIC AWARENESS AND TRAINING

Education, public awareness and training interact with a variety of areas in Agenda 21, the Tbilisi Intergovernmental Conference on Environmental Education in 1977 'provided fundamental principles ..'..

Basic **education** should be available to everybody, of particular concern is the low access for girls and women: targets were set for primary education for 80 % of girls and boys and halving the adult illiteracy rate, but without mentioning a target date. Improved formal and non-formal education should contribute to enhance awareness for sustainable development. Environment and development should be integrated into educational activities, it is needed as a 'cross-cutting issue' from school to adult education, for employees and in universities, further training, for decisionmakers and employees. Relevant methods and material should be developed for environmental education programmes.

Through **public awareness** campaigning, the understanding of human interference into nature should be strengthened. Public information services on environment and development, eg. information of modern communication technologies and audio-visual methods, should be made available. Cultural and journalistic activities with regard to environment and development should be strengthened. Awareness initiatives should involve a variety of groups, including indigenous people, children and women; their activities and those of other NGOs should be encouraged.

Vocational **training** programmes should address issues of environment and development and 'fill gaps in knowledge and skill that would help individuals find employment'. Future needs should be introduced in workforce training to enable them to deal with environment and development problems. Managerial concern should be enhanced on environmental problems and environmental management applied. A variety of groups, including professional associations, trade unions and employers' organisations should integrate environment and development issues into their activities. Primary environmental care and services of environmental technicians should be provided, particularly in deprived areas.

*Apart from financial terms, this uncontroversial chapter arrived in Rio without brackets.*

## CHAPTER 37: NATIONAL MECHANISMS AND INTERNATIONAL COOPERATION FOR CAPACITY-BUILDING

Capacity-building seeks to enhance the capabilities of countries for the implementation of sustainable development, allowing a broad participation of non-governmental organisations. Endogenous capacity-building involves individuals and institutions, science and technology, skills and expertise, NGOs and research centres, municipalities and governments, universities and business. International cooperation is here a major approach, but the priorities are to be provided locally. Technical cooperation including technology transfer and skills process should re-orient towards local needs and conditions. National capacity-building strategies and programmes are to be developed for implementation of Agenda 21. Sectoral strategies should be considered and review mechanisms should be implemented. The UN system should strengthen their capacity-building activities, multilateral development institutions should improve their environmental responsibilities and should ensure the integration of environment and development; environmental impact should be assessed throughout and regional coordination and harmonisation should be considered. By 1994 or earlier, countries should review their capacity-building requirements and the UN Secretary-General should report by 1997 on implementation of technical cooperation, its achievements and further activities still needed. A national consensus on capacity-building strategies should be built. UNDP is the major international body concerned with capacity-building. It could assist in meeting needs for technical cooperation and on the national planning process, it should provide assistance through its field offices. Review mechanisms on capacity-building and technical cooperation should be established.

*Capacity-building is a crucial concept in Agenda 21, referring to the institutional capacities and networks which are required to enable countries effectively to integrate environment and development concerns. It deals with assistance to national planning processes and regional review mechanisms, financial resources and gathering and analysis of environmental and developmental data, and not only with the fieldwork of specific projects. In focusing on activities at local and national level, this chapter is complementary to the next chapter on international institutions. The chapter stresses the leading role for UNDP and its field offices in assisting countries upon request with such capacity-building, but is ambiguous concerning the resource requirements and institutional implications for UNDP itself.*

## CHAPTER 38: INTERNATIONAL INSTITUTIONAL ARRANGEMENTS

The **UN system**[15] is considered as the major body concerning the UNCED follow-up. The restructuring and revitalisation of the UN system is supported. Work on sustainable development shall be strengthened. Cooperation on relevant issues within the UN system and with other organisations should be promoted. Follow-up measures on review of implementation and on institutional arrangements shall be ensured.

' The **General Assembly** ... is the principal policy-making and appraisal organ on matters relating to the follow-up of UNCED'. The implementation of Agenda 21 is to be reviewed regularly, 'a special session ... [on] overall review and appraisal of Agenda 21' could be held 'no later than 1997'.

The revitalisation of the **UN Economic and Social Council (ECOSOC)** is supported. The Council should 'overview ... the implementation of Agenda 21' and should undertake 'system-wide coordination and integration of environmental and developmental aspects in the United Nations' policies and programmes'. It should make relevant recommendations and review the work of the CSD periodically.

A 'high-level **Commission on Sustainable Development** (CSD) should be established ..'.. The commission should 'ensure the effective follow-up of the Conference, ... enhance international cooperation and rationalize the intergovernmental decision-making capacity for the integration of environment and development issues and ... examine the progress of the implementation of

---

[15]For details of the immediate UN follow-up to Chapter 38, see Part I, Section 3.4 in this book.

Agenda 21 at the national, regional and international levels'. It should 'monitor progress in the implementation of Agenda 21' and analyse and evaluate activities in the UN system on environment and development. It should consider information provided by governments and review progress, both on implementation of Agenda 21 and other UNCED agreements and on problems, such as financing and technology transfer. Dialogue with NGOs should be enhanced and relevant work of NGOs should be analysed. It is a functional commission of ECOSOC, to 'report to the Economic and Social Council ... vis-a-vis the General Assembly', and should 'provide appropriate recommendations to the General Assembly, through the Economic and Social Council ..'.. The Commission 'would consist of representatives of States elected as members with due regard to equitable geographical distribution', non-members states would send observers. It 'should provide for active involvement of [UN bodies], international financial institutions and other relevant intergovernmental organizations'. Participation of NGOs, including industry, business and science, should be encouraged. Specific measures on membership etc. were postponed for the General Assembly at its 47th session (Autumn 1992). The Commission should meet for the first time no later than 1993.

High-level coordination of relevant activities within the UN system should be undertaken by the revitalised **Administrative Committee on Coordination (ACC)**. It 'should consider establishing a .. special .. subcommittee.. ' and should 'provide a vital link and interface between the multilateral financial institutions and other United Nations bodies at the highest administrative level'.

A high-level **advisory body** on environment and development should be established. It should consist of eminent persons appointed by the UN Secretary-General. 'A highly qualified and competent **secretariat** support structure within the United Nations Secretariat' should be established. It 'should provide support to the work of both intergovernmental and interagency coordination mechanisms'.

The following **UN organs, programmes and organisations** should play their relevant part in the implementation of Agenda 21:

- The role of **UNEP** is to be enhanced and strengthened, by working as a catalyst within the UN system and stimulating international activities, international legal material, environmental monitoring and data dissemination, and environmental impact assessments. Initiatives at regional and sub-regional level should be supported, and advice should be made available to governments, particularly on the integration of environment into development.

- The **UNDP** is given a 'crucial role in the follow-up', it will coordinate aid and advise on implementation of Agenda 21 with appropriate participation of NGOs. UNDP is 'acting as the lead agency in ... capacity-building at local, national and regional level', 'mobilizing donor resources ... for capacity-building ... and , where appropriate, through the use of UNDP round-table mechanisms'; 'strengthening its own programmes ..' ., 'assisting recipient countries, upon request, [in] ... national coordination mechanisms and networks to activities for the follow-up of UNCED [and] ... in coordinating the mobilization of domestic financial resources'; 'promoting and strengthening the role and involvement of women, youth and other major groups ..' ..

- **UNCTAD** 'should play an important role in the implementation of Agenda 21 ... [and] take into account the importance of the interrelationships between development, international trade and the environment ..' ..

- The **UN Sudano-Sahelian Office** should coordinate activities on drought, desertification and land resource management

- UN specialised agencies, related organizations and relevant intergovernmental organisations should adjust their programmes and activities to contribute to the implementation of the UNCED agreements.

**Regional and sub-regional cooperation** needs to be strengthened. Regional economic commissions should coordinate regional and sub-regional activities and provide assistance to countries on sustainable development. Collaboration among regional commissions, regional development banks, NGOs and other institutions at regional level is needed. UNEP, UNDP and regional commissions will provide assistance in national capacity-building. UNEP and UNDP should strengthen their cooperation on environmental issues of development projects. Regional intergovernmental technical and economic organisations should coordinate activities on environmental problems of regional significance. On action to combat drought and desertification, regional and sub-regional organizations should be the major actors, assisted by UNEP, UNDP and UN Statistical Office (UNSO). Regional and sub-regional organisations and relevant UN organisations should strengthen their cooperation.

'**States** have an important role to play in the follow-up of UNCED and the implementation of Agenda 21'. States 'could consider the preparation' of national reports and national action plans for the implementation of Agenda 21.

Upon request, policies and the preparation of national strategies and reports should be assisted and supported by UN institutions, in particular by UNDP. A national coordination structure may be established. Existing assistance consortia, consultative groups and round tables should strengthen their activities towards integration of environment into developmental strategies.

Because a successful implementation needs 'an effective link between substantive action and financial support', a 'close and effective **cooperation** between **United Nations bodies** and the **multilateral financial organizations**' is required. The international financial institutions should be actively involved in the international deliberations.

**Non-governmental organisations** and major groups have an important role in the implementation of Agenda 21. The follow-up process should be 'open and effective'. The participation of NGOs in the review and evaluation process should be achieved and their contribution promoted, their findings should be taken into account. Support for southern NGOs and their networks should be provided. NGOs should have access to reports and other UN information. The 'proposal to establish a non-governmental Earth Council and the proposal to appoint a guardian for future generations' are 'noted'.

*The success of the follow-up is much dependent upon the improved functioning of UN institutions. From a variety of proposals, the CSD gradually won support as the major follow-up institution. Its relationship to ECOSOC and the UN General Assembly led to considerable discussion at Rio. While the African countries wanted a strong commission reporting to the UN General Assembly, others including the UK and India sought other options. Brazil lobbied to weaken the language on national development plans, Egypt and other African countries, and some Asian countries, supported a stronger process; language on the national reporting system and national action plans was weakened to 'could consider the preparation ..'.. Several developing countries proposed that these plans and reports could be used as a basis for demanding missing financial and technical resources.*

## CHAPTER 39: INTERNATIONAL LEGAL INSTRUMENTS AND MECHANISMS

'The overall objective of the review and development of international environmental law should be to evaluate and to promote the efficacy of that law and to promote the integration of environment and development policies through effective international agreements or instruments, taking into account both universal principles and the particular and differentiated needs and concerns of all countries'.

Effective participation, particularly of developing countries, in the negotiations of international agreements should be strengthened, technical and financial assistance to improve national capabilities should be provided. 'Effective, full and prompt implementation' of legal material should be ensured, relevant mechanisms including review of reporting systems should be considered, recognising the special needs of developing countries. Difficulties of countries in the participation and implementation of international agreements should be addressed. Specific measures may consider general rights and obligations of states, including environmental destruction during armed conflicts. The development of a nuclear safety convention is supported. International environmental standards and less restrictive trade policies are considered as most favourable environmental policy measures. Methods and techniques for the avoidance and settlement of disputes, particularly those related to environment and development should be strengthened.

*The purpose of this chapter appears to be to strengthen the procedures concerning the participation in and implementation of international legal agreements on environment and development. The major concern of developing countries was the creation of international environmental law without their participation. The most contentious paragraph concerned the 'environmental crimes' provision. While the EC preferred a general approach for times of both peace and war, the USA and many G77 countries successfully argued that it should be valid only during war.*

## CHAPTER 40: INFORMATION FOR DECISIONMAKING

Decisionmaking for sustainable development needs more relevant information on a wide variety of sectors.

Neither GNP nor measurements of resource flows or pollution in current use, provide an adequate guide to sustainability, so appropriate indicators of sustainable development need to be developed at national and international levels. These indicators should be harmonised, updated regularly and used globally; relevant international capacities are to be strengthened. Collection and assessment of data should be strengthened particularly in developing countries to 'bridge the **data gap**'; data transformation and coordination should be improved to achieve a more useful and comprehensive insight. Of concern is the weakness of information on development issues. The accessibility of information needed for planning, decisionmaking and private use should be improved. The methodology of information collection and assessment, including computer-systems etc. should be harmonised and developed. Traditional knowledge should be included in information collection activities, relevant information should be provided to local communities.

The collected and assessed information is not of much use unless it is made available and exchanged properly. The **availability of information** should be strengthened and equitable access should be ensured, and the needs of decisionmakers and particular user groups should be addressed. Information documentation systems should be developed and strengthened, networking and electronic links should be encouraged particularly to allow those yet unserved to participate. Information handling and communication should be strengthened on the national level, and in particular developing countries should improve their national capacities and their international participation should be ensured.

*Without further discussion this chapter was easily adopted at Rio.*

## 9.6 Agenda 21: Central themes and implementation

Agenda 21 presents a masterplan of action for sustainable development throughout the world. Just about any issue related to environment and development receives mention. It is not legally binding, but nor is it simply the product of a committee of experts or commission; it is a negotiated document agreed among more than 150 governments. What general themes are then revealed by this huge international effort, and how may it be implemented?

**Underlying themes**
One theme which emerges clearly is a 'bottom-up' approach which places the emphasis on people, communities, and non-government organisations. For example, the chapter on poverty emphasises the need to address the basic needs of the poor, to improve their education and strengthen their opportunities and participation in local governance. This contrasts with previous emphasis on

international sponsorship of great public projects intended to boost local economies and generate wealth and employment through the expenditure and resulting supply of cheap resources, such as big electricity projects. Disillusion with such grand project-oriented planning is evident throughout Agenda 21. This critical attitude towards a 'top-down' approach reflects in part the enhanced participation of NGOs in the PrepCom negotiations.

In a similar vein, the role of 'community participation' in sustainable development is highlighted, and the role of women in local decisionmaking receives repeated emphasis, as does the need to acknowledge and respect indigenous peoples and their knowledge. Such references appear in several chapters of Agenda 21, and relevant groups each have a particular chapter in the major groups section. Local expertise and traditional knowledge (particularly concerning sustainable use of biological resources) is to be valued and incorporated in sustainable development plans and measures, and the voices of indigenous and other local communities should be heard when economic developments conflict with their interests. Many such references arose through the influence of non-governmental groups working on their national delegates, and sometimes drafting text which became incorporated in Agenda 21.

In keeping with this, there is significant emphasis on the need for 'open governance': participatory democracy, transparency, accountability, etc. Such references seem to have received little opposition, even from those countries which clearly do not practice such principles. Agenda 21 thus seems to represent on paper the much-vaunted global triumph of the ideals of participatory democracy.

Lack of adequate knowledge and institutions, both within countries and internationally, is seen as a key obstacle to implementing Agenda 21, particularly but not exclusively with respect to the developing countries. Almost every chapter highlights a need for greater knowledge and understanding, and in keeping with the bottom-up approach, sustainable development requires adequate education and development of the 'human resources' required to transform the ideas into reality. Some governments also lack the institutional means required to enact some of the policies in Agenda 21. There is in consequence a persistent need for 'capacity-building', and for international assistance in achieving this.

Agenda 21 emphasises the need for integrated approaches, along two main themes. It really does seek to integrate environment and development, with environment and development issues inextricably entwined; much of the financial requirements, for example, are related to intrinsic development objectives of poverty alleviation, human settlements etc. Also, Agenda 21 tries to integrate different disciplines and sectors towards a more comprehensive approach. This can be found for scientific research where interdisciplinary activities should be strengthened as well as for policy and politics where integrated environmentally sound management of resources should be adopted and cooperation and coordination of sectoral decisionmaking strengthened. As long as only the environment and development ministries recognise the need for political changes, the effort is likely to fail. The entire decisionmaking processes at all levels should be oriented towards policy adjustments. Existing institutions need strengthened coordination and cooperation between various sectors and different levels (ie. local, national, international).

Was there a defeat for regulation and a victory for market mechanisms, as some claimed? The relevant chapters (eg. Chapter 8 on decisionmaking processes) suggest a more complex outcome. Compared to other international environmental agreements, in Agenda 21 the recognition of environmental pricing and fiscal/economic policies is far stronger than previously common. Regulation sets an 'effective legal and regulatory framework' and 'integrated, enforceable and effective laws', while market mechanisms should have a 'complementary role'. It is not a question of replacing one approach by the other but adopting both and enhancing their mutual effect.

In general the role and responsibilities of business receive a low and ambiguous profile in Agenda 21. In the run-up to UNCED, there was considerable activity in this area, and various approaches were advanced, as outlined in section 4.6 of this report. The approach implied in Agenda 21 is much closer to that of self-regulation, as advocated by the International Chamber of Commerce and (less exclusively) by the Business Council for Sustainable Development (BCSD), than more explicit internationally-negotiated codes of conduct and environmental reporting as advanced by the former UN Centre on Transnational Corporations.

This is arguably one of several issues not adequately addressed in Agenda 21. Other near-absent issues include the environmental and developmental impacts of conflict and militarism; nuclear facilities; and, international debt. In general there are clear political reasons why these were kept off the agenda as being either too divisive, or as issues being addressed in other fora - or both.

### Finance and implementation

As stated in the Preamble, governments carry the primary responsibility for implementing Agenda 21. They agreed the document and have the means to develop the regulatory measures required, and are the relevant authorities to decide upon national and international financial disbursement.

In practice is is inevitable that although nearly all governments did participate in the negotiations and agree the final text, they will vary considerably in the seriousness with which they take the exercise, and in their readiness to accept and act upon the ideas embodied in Agenda 21. Yet many other actors will be involved. Local authorities often manage resources like water, waste etc; their sectoral policies could be adjusted, affected also by increased participation of citizen and local groups. Industry needs to examine relevant chapters, such as those on wastes and chemicals, closely. NGOs will have to address a strengthened role in decisionmaking. And a range of UN and other international bodies will be expected to take full account of relevant recommendations for action. Those who pushed so hard to change attitudes and language in Agenda 21 will have to continue their efforts if the language of the document is to be translated into reality.

To oversee such implementation, the CSD is created as the major international follow-up institution, whilst the UNDP and its field offices will play a key role in assisting and supporting countries on capacity-building and other activities related to sustainable development. Governments can develop strategies for implementing Agenda 21 and report progress to the CSD. Whether they will depends upon their perceptions and priorities, as affected by public pressure within a country and whether local and provincial authorities implement sustainable development and/or NGOs campaign on these issues. The Commission will have some powers to examine and review national action, but many countries particularly in the North need to commit themselves to undertake action and to communicate with the Commission to get the implementation of Agenda 21 going and to get also the more reluctant countries on board.

This may well be an area of some difficulty and disappointment. Not only is the reporting process not binding, but it is only loosely specified, whilst the review process in very unclear. Unless the CSD or governments themselves can develope and coordinate a fairly clear and standard way of presenting information, the CSD will be faced with the task of reviewing and interpreting potentially more than a hundred national reports, of variable scope, and all in different forms and addressing different aspects of issues at different levels. This may not be only difficult but messy, bureaucratic and contentious. Unless clearer procedures and purposes can be developed and accepted, the main value of national reports may be the national benefits gained from the process of developing them, rather than any structured international comparison or review.

Developing countries may also use reporting upon their national plans as a way of estimating needs for financial resources and the transfer of technology. The issue of finance was a recurring sore in the Agenda 21 negotiations. As indicated, each programme area was given a price tag by the UNCED secretariat. These numbers are summarised in Appendix 1, and amount to about $600bn/yr over the rest of the decade, with an estimated requirement for $125bn/yr in aid or loans to developing countries on concessional terms, spread broadly across a wide range of programme areas. Coincidentally, this corresponds roughly to the UN goal for ODA of 0.7% of GNP from rich countries. To this extent, the financial estimates in Agenda 21 help to explain what the 0.7% figure could be used for.

As also indicated in Appendix 1, it is clear that the amounts available through intergovernmental transfers are almost unchanged after UNCED, at just under half this total. There seems little prospect of these amounts being greatly increased. Given the repeated statements from developing countries that the implementation of Agenda 21 is wholly dependent upon additional finance being made available, this places major constraints on its global implementation. It remains to be seen whether developing countries will react to this reality by renouncing Agenda 21, or by adopting the aspects which they can reasonably pursue without additional resources, and the consequent implications of this for the pursuit of globally sustainable development.

To conclude, Agenda 21 serves as the most extensive guidebook to sustainable development ever prepared. The fact that it was negotiated by governments, drawing on a much broader participatory process, has done a great deal to inform those involved in myriad ways, and to clarify the nature of the underlying conflicts of interest and difficulties in implementing sustainable development. Agenda 21 will serve as a reference book of ideas, principles and approaches for many years to come. Whether it has achieved any more is, as yet, an open question.

# Chapter 10

## Forest Principles

Francis Sullivan
WorldWide Fund for Nature, UK

Full title:
*'Non-legally binding authoritative statement of principles
for a global consensus on the management, conservation
and sustainable development of all types of forests'*
(UNCED A/CONF.151/6/Rev.1)

## 10.1 Origins of the Forest Principles

It was not until the early 1980s that serious concerns were voiced about the state of the world's forests. Assessments by the Food and Agricultural Organisation of the United Nations (FAO) showed that the tropical forests were disappearing a rate of over 11 million hectares a year.

The effects of deforestation could be seen in economic, social and environmental terms, but research showed that a range of factors were responsible, including poverty, debt, trade, high population growth rates, landlessness, inappropriate policy planning and poor forestry practices. To solve the problem would therefore need a broad based and concerted effort.

During the early 1980s, a number of unilateral and multilateral responses were proposed: FAO joined forces with the World Bank, UNDP and the World Resources Institute and launched the Tropical Forestry Action Plan (TFAP), while the International Tropical Timber Organisation (ITTO) was established under the auspices of UNCTAD. These efforts were government-led, and assumed that the causes of deforestation lay within the forestry sector.

Moreover, during the late 1980s, it became increasingly clear that the response to tropical deforestation had not succeeded in slowing the rates of forest loss. Criticism of the TFAP (and later the ITTO) grew, as NGOs voiced their concerns that the organisations which had been set up to halt tropical deforestation were doing little to change land use on the ground and in some cases proposed scenarios which would have increased forest loss.

In early 1990, FAO repeated its tropical forest survey. The results were shocking: during the 1980s rates of tropical deforestation had increased by over 50%. Efforts to stem the tide of deforestation had simply failed.

Again, proposals were made on how the problem of tropical deforestation could be solved. Many argued that a heavy-weight organisation would be needed to make countries accountable for protecting their forests - but how could this be done?

Also emerging at the end of the 1980s was a movement away from talking about *tropical* forests in isolation. Evidence that the world's natural temperate and boreal forests were also under threat (and retreating) led to the idea that what was needed was a 'global forest agreement' which would require all the world's governments to commit to looking after their own forests and ensuring that their national policies did not promote the misuse of forests overseas.

The concept of a Global Forest Convention was first mooted in the Report of the Independent Review of the TFAP in May 1990. The idea was picked up at the G7 meeting in Houston later that year, and spread fast, particularly in the developed world, where ironically, concerns about tropical deforestation were greatest. FAO was quick to latch onto the concept and work was initiated on preparing a first rough draft of a forest convention. Further fuel was added to the debate when HRH Prince of Wales made a specific reference to the need for a global forest convention at a meeting in London in 1990.

Efforts were also being made to develop binding agreements to protect biological diversity and limit climate change. So it seemed logical that three conventions should be put forward to signature in Rio.

By this stage, warning bells were starting to ring in governments of the tropical nations. It appeared to them that the efforts to draw up a global forest convention (so strongly promoted by Northern nations) were little more than a mechanism to prevent them from developing their forests in the way they wished to. Developing nations also viewed the forest convention as a mechanism for the North to duck the main issue of reducing greenhouse gas emissions. There was widespread and open opposition throughout the tropical countries to any form of legally binding agreement on forests.

Throughout the UNCED process it was clear that there was no consensus on how to manage wisely the world's forests. Initial attempts to launch negotiations on a convention were rapidly transformed into discussions on a set of 'Principles for Forest Management', and repeated attempts to elevate this into negotiations on a convention failed in the face of adamant opposition from several key developing countries. Governments from tropical countries spoke out very powerfully against the concept that the rest of the world should have the right to lecture them about how to manage their forests. After all how many temperate countries have successfully conserved a high proportion of their native forest? The South was simply not prepared to be told what to do with their forests even if they were offered compensation by the North.

Within the overall position of the South, there were a range of views. Brazil argued that any international intervention in its internal affairs was out of the question, however Malaysia was calling for a commitment that all countries should preserve 30% of their territory under forests or provide the funds to do it elsewhere (see also Section 4.5).

The deadlock was never really broken in Rio, and the resulting document, the 'Forest Principles', with its most unwieldy title, bears the scars of what became a very difficult negotiation. The discussion was not about forests, forestry or even sustainable management, but much more to do with international politics and sovereignty.

## 10.2 Analysis of the text

The mass of drafting and redrafting which took place before the Forest Principles could be agreed at Rio makes logical analysis difficult, if not impossible. The text is repetitive and regressive, clumsy and at times contradictory. The title of the Forest Principles is significant. The document clearly covers *all* forests, not only tropical forests. No other forest agreement to date has considered all the forests of the world.

The Forest Principles are divided into two sections, Preamble and Principles/ Elements. The Preamble comprises eight short sections which set the scene and define the scope of the document: that the world's forests are important for economic, social and environmental reasons and they should therefore be used by humans in such a way that the goods and services provided by forests should not be reduced over time.

The Principles/Elements are divided into 15 sections. Rather than attempting to analyse the text section by section, this chapter picks out the five themes which run through the text and to refer the reader to specific sections where appropriate.

**1. Importance and roles of forests**. Throughout the text, implicit and explicit reference is made to the importance of forests, not only for the tangible goods they supply, but also for the services they provide. **Section 2b** states that forests should be sustainably managed to meet social, economic, ecological, cultural and spiritual needs and lists the range of forest products, goods and services which humans benefit from:

'...wood and wood products, water, food, fodder, medicine, fuel, shelter, employment, recreation, habitats for wildlife, landscape diversity, carbon sinks and reservoirs, and for other forest products'.

**Section 4** also stresses the importance of forests in maintaining ecological processes, protecting watersheds, storing biological diversity and providing genetic material for the biotechnology industry. No reference is made to the ongoing reduction in the capability of the world's forest to supply these benefits, but the need to control pollution as it affects forests is made in **Section 15**. However, the text does refer specifically to the importance of protecting old growth forests and maintaining ecological integrity, **Sections 8e and f**.

**Sections 6a and d** mention the importance of forests as providers of energy. Reference is made to the need to establish plantations to provide for fuel and industrial wood requirements.

**2. Need for action and international cooperation.** Although the scale of the world's forest problems is not stated, the majority of sections of the text refer to the need for national and international action to promote the 'management, conservation and sustainable development of forests'. For example, **Section 3a** refers to the need for 'increased efforts ..'. for the management, conservation and sustainable development of forests and forest lands. There is also clear reference to the fact that an integrated approach is required; ie. by not focusing only on the forestry sector, **Section 3c, 9c and 13d**.

The need for action, particularly by developed countries is stressed in **Section 8a**. The range of afforestation, reforestation and forest rehabilitation measures are mentioned in **Section 8b** with the aim of maintaining and increasing forest cover. Other sections are more specific about the sorts of 'efforts' required:

i) Funds/debt reduction. **Section 1b** states that the full cost of managing forests sustainably should be borne by the international community. **Section 7a** calls for a 'supportive international economic climate' to promote sustainable patterns of consumption, to eradicate poverty and promote food security. **Section 7b** follows this with a call for funds to help developing nations establish programmes for the conservation of forests, including protected natural forest. The text is littered with other specific references to the need to increase levels of funding and reduce the debts of developing nations; calling for, 'financial and technical cooperation'

**Section 8c**, 'reduction of external indebtedness' **Section 9a**; 'eradication of poverty' **Section 9b**; and 'new and additional financial resources' **Section 10**.

ii) Trade. Broadly, the Principles favour free trade: 'Trade in forest products should be based on non-discriminatory and multilaterally agreed rules and procedures consistent with international trade law and practices'. In this context, open and free international trade in forest products should be facilitated, **Section 13a**. They also specifically call for tariff removals, improved market access, better prices and local production **Section 13b**. However, **Section 13e** appears contradictory calling for intervention in areas where trade policy leads to forest degradation: 'Fiscal, trade, industrial, transportation and other policies and practices that may lead to forest degradation should be avoided'. But **Section 14** counters that with, 'Unilateral measures, incompatible with international obligations or agreements, to restrict and/or ban international trade in timber or other forest products should be removed or avoided, in order to attain long-term sustainable forest management'.

iii) Assessments and guidelines. Little mention is made of the need to avoid unsustainable use of forests. However, the need for Environmental Impact Assessments (EIAs) is made in **Section 8h**. The formulation of guidelines for sustainable forest management is also encouraged, **Section 8d**.

iv) Training and technology transfer. References are made to the need for improved technology transfer, **Section 11**, research **Section 12a**, information exchange **Section 12c** and for this information to be equitably shared **Section 12d**. A call for institution building in education, training, science, technology, economics, anthropology and social aspects of forests and forest management is made in **Section 12b**.

**3. Local participation. Sections 2c and d** stress the need to inform the public and provide an opportunity for the participation of interested parties, involving:

'...local communities and indigenous people, industries, labour, non-governmental organizations and individuals, forest dwellers and women, in the development, implementation and planning of national forest policies'.

Although a very broad wish-list, this section provides a yardstick to judge whether governments have sought the views of specific interested groups.

**Section 5a** reaffirms the importance of local people in conserving forests:

'National forest policies should recognize and duly support the identity, culture and the rights of indigenous people, their communities and other communities and forest dwellers'.

This section goes on to stress the importance of secure land tenure, the maintenance of cultural diversity and social organisation. **Section 5b** stresses the importance of the full participation of women in the management, conservation and sustainable management of forests. These considerations are not central to the paper and the form of words is so weak that it will not have any real impact at the national level.

**4. National Sovereignty.** The sovereignty message comes across strongly and repeatedly. **Section 1a** states that although governments have the right to exploit the forests within their national boundaries, they have a responsibility to ensure that their activities do not negatively affect other countries. In the case of forests, this could refer to increased river siltation levels, the production of carbon dioxide by forest clearance or the loss of biological diversity. However, **Section 2a** reaffirms the principle of sovereignty, stressing the right of each country to set its development priorities and to decide which areas of forest should be converted to other land use.

It seems incongruous that nations should have the sovereign right to develop their forests as they please, if they are then invited to approach the international community to help them pay for managing their forests sustainably.

**5. Full economic valuation.** The text makes several references to the full economic valuation of forests. For instance, **Section 6c** calls for 'comprehensive assessment of economic and non-economic values of forest goods and services and of the environmental costs and benefits. The development and improvement of methodologies for such evaluations should be promoted'. **Section 13c** calls for environmental costs and benefits to be included into market forces.

## 10.3 Implications and prospects
The fact that this is a **non-legally binding** document coupled with the lack of a logical layout and the repetitive nature of the text means that it is not clear

what governments are expected to do. Governments will interpret the text to suit their own objectives, and therefore, this document may be used to support 'business as usual', or worse weaken a number of the international commitments already made.

The text is relatively 'top-down', with strong emphasis upon the role of government and decision making by government. Nevertheless it acknowledges that a wide variety of interest groups should be informed about the state of a nation's forests and given an opportunity to participate in the development, implementation and planning of national forest policies.

Although the Forest Principles make no clear reference to the *precautionary principle*, the *polluter pays principle*, targets, the need for cost internalisation in forestry or biological diversity, various sections of the text make it clear that it is the responsibility of governments to ensure that the management of a nation's forests is socially beneficial and ecologically benign. The key topics are summarised as follows:

* Importance of forests to meet human needs and maintain ecological processes (2b,4,8e).
* Need to protection old growth forests (8f).
* Provision of fuelwood (6a,6d).
* Need for an integrated approach (3c,9c,13d).
* Need for action at national and international levels (3a,8a,8b). Specifically: i) Funds/debt reduction (1b,7a,7b,8c,9b,10); ii) Trade (13a,13b,13e,14); iii) Guidelines (8d,8h); iv) Training and institution building (11,12a,12b,12c,12d).
* Local participation (2c,2d,5a,5b).
* Role of women (5b).
* National sovereignty (1a,2a).
* Full economic evaluation (6c,13c).
* Pollution and forests (2b,15).

As a minimum response to signing up to the Forest Principles, individual governments could be expected to carry out a number of actions:

* Establish a high-level cross-departmental working party to draw up an integrated forest policy, binding on all government departments to increase efforts to protect and sustainably manage forests and woodlands within the country, linked to overseas aid and trade policy (1a, 3a,7a, 7b, 8a, 8b, 8c, 8e, 8f, 3c, 6b, 9a, 9b, 9c, 10, 13d, 15).

- Establish a mechanism to provide opportunities for the participation of interested parties, including local communities and indigenous peoples, industries, labour, NGOs and individuals, forest dwellers and women, in the development, implementation and planning of national forest policies (2c, 2d, 5a, 5b, 6d).

- Help to create a strengthened multilateral legislation to protect forests which are under threat from inappropriate fiscal, trade, industrial and transportation policies (13e).

Thus, the Principles can be used by organisations which are working on issues such as debt reduction, increased project funding, conversion of old growth forests, trade, participation of tribal and local people. Many believe that in itself this document will be able to do little, but may form the basis both for non-government work, and for more meaningful international cooperation at a later stage.

## 10.4 Conclusions

UNCED failed to reach a 'minimum' agreement on a forward-looking statement of principles that would have recognised the interconnections between forests and issues such as biological diversity and climate change, as well as recognising the role of forests within a broader land-use context. Nevertheless, many believe it was a miracle that the Forest Principles were agreed in Rio, considering the range of views between states and the short time period available for negotiation.

Agreement was eventually achieved by a process of avoiding specific commitments or contentious principles, and incorporating a wide range of generalised observations, recommendations and goals, sometimes in themselves ambiguous or perhaps contradictory. The result is a document with something for everyone, without any clear message or direction.

Although to many the Forest Principles are disappointing in that they fail to provide a legal instrument for stimulating the protection and improved management of the world's forests, they do provide a framework which can be used to hold national governments to a number of principles. Mere acceptance of the need for some form of international cooperation on forests was for some developing countries a substantial psychological step.

Thus, the negotiations on the Forest Principles highlight the formidable obstacles to achieving an effective convention on forests, but nevertheless do represent a modest step forward towards an international regime for forest management.

# Appendix 1

## Financial estimates, pledges and likely resources

To many negotiators and commentators involved in the UNCED process, financial issues were of absolute central importance. Debates over the control and indicative levels of finance, especially that provided for developing countries from the developed economies, formed some of the most heated and protracted debates in negotiation of both the Conventions, and of Agenda 21.

### Financial estimates and requirements

Both the Conventions established the principle that developing countries should be refunded the 'full agreed incremental costs' associated with measures taken under them, with the GEF, administered by the World Bank in conjunction with UNEP and UNDP as the interim funding mechanism. Whether and how the concept of 'full agreed incremental cost' can ever be defined, given the recognition that environmental protection and development are inextricably intertwined, remains to be seen. In the Conventions, no specific figures were mentioned. However, there was clear expectation on the part of developing countries at least that the GEF would be expanded far beyond the pilot phase (1990-93) level of around US$300m/yr[1] as it moves into the operational phase for implementing the Conventions.

Agenda 21, by contrast, adopted a different approach. It stated that 'substantial new and additional funding for sustainable development and implementation of Agenda 21 will be required' (A21:33.15), and that 'the cost of inaction could outweigh the financial costs of implementing Agenda 21. Inaction will narrow the choices of future generations' (A21:33.4).

In an attempt to clarify the needs, the Secretariat provided estimates of the costs associated with each programme area, as summarised in Table 1. These estimates were arrived at by various means. In a few areas, such as population and water, detailed estimates had already been agreed in international fora and could be incorporated. In some areas, the Secretariat made estimates based upon detailed commissioned studies. For many areas, however, the Secretariat had to make crude estimates based simply upon discussion and general principles relating to the scale of different sectors and order of magnitude estimates of the additional costs which Agenda 21 activities might incur. Supporting documents for the estimates are incomplete, and there was no critical review of them. Consequently the numbers were cited in Agenda 21

---

[1] All figures can be considered as 1990 US dollars unless otherwise stated.

with due qualification that:

'The secretariat of the Conference has estimated the average total annual cost (1993-2000) of implementing the activities of this programme to be about ..., including about ... from the international community on grant or concessional terms. These are indicative and order of magnitude estimates only and have not been reviewed by Governments. Actual costs and financial terms, including any that are non-concessional, will depend upon, *inter alia*, the specific strategies and programmes Governments decide upon for implementation'.

**Table 1:** Estimated total average annual cost for implementing Agenda 21 programmes.

| Chapter / Programme Area | Total cost for developing countries (US$m/yr) | incl. grant or concessional requirement (US$m/yr) |
|---|---|---|
| **2. International trade and national economic policies** | | |
| A. trade liberalization | | 8,800 |
| B. trade and environment mutually supportive | - | - |
| C. financial resources to developing countries and debt | incl. in Ch.33 | incl. in Ch.33 |
| D. national economic policies | | 50 |
| **3. Poverty** | 30,000 | 15,000 |
| **4. Consumption patterns** | - | - |
| **5. Population** | | |
| A. links to sustainable development | - | - |
| B. national policies | | 90 |
| C. programmes at local level | 7,000 | 3,500 |
| **6. Human health** | | |
| A. primary health care | 40,000 | 5,000 |
| B. communicable diseases | 4,000 | 900 |
| C. vulnerable groups | 3,700 | 400 |
| D. urban health | 222 | 22 |
| E. environmental pollution and hazards | 3,000 | 115 |
| **7. Human settlement** | | |
| A. adequate shelter | 75,000 | 10,000 |
| B. human settlement management | 100,000 | 15,000 |
| C. land-use planning and management | 3,000 | 300 |
| D. environmental infrastructure | | 50 |
| E. energy and transport systems | incl. in Ch. 9 | incl. in Ch. 9 |
| F. disaster-prone areas | | 50 |
| G. construction industry | 40,000 | 40,000 |
| H. human resource development and capacity-building | | 65 |

| Chapter / Programme Area | Total cost for developing countries (US$m/yr) | incl. grant or concessional requirement (US$m/yr) |
|---|---|---|
| **8. Integration in decisionmaking** | | |
| A. policy, planning and management | | 50 |
| B. legal and regulatory framework | | 6 |
| C. economic instruments and market incentives | | 5 |
| D. integrated environmental and economic accounting | | 2 |
| **9. Atmosphere** | | |
| A. scientific work | | 640 |
| B. energy, transportation, industry, terrestrial and marine resources | | 20,000 |
| C. stratospheric ozone depletion | | |
| D. transboundary atmospheric pollution | | 160-590 |
| **10. Land resources** | | 50 |
| **11. Deforestation** | | |
| A. multiple roles and functions of forests | 2,500 | 860 |
| B. protection and conservation | 10,000 | 3,700 |
| C. forestry goods and services | 18,000 | 880 |
| D. planning, assessment and systematic observation | 750 | 530 |
| **12. Desertification and drought** | | |
| A. knowledge, information and knowledge base | 350 | 175 |
| B. combating land degradation | 6,000 | 3,000 |
| C. integrated development programmes | incl.in Ch.3,14 | incl.in Ch.3,14 |
| D. comprehensive anti-desertification programmes | 180 | 90 |
| E. drought preparedness and drought relief | 1,200 | 1,100 |
| F. popular participation and environmental education | 1,000 | 500 |
| **13. Mountain** | | |
| A. knowledge | | 50 |
| B. integrated watershed development | 13,000 | 1,900 |
| **14. Agriculture** | | |
| A. policy review, planning and integrated programming | 3,000 | 450 |
| B. people's participation and human resource development | 4,400 | 650 |
| C. diversification of farming systems | | |
| D. land resource planning, information and education | 10,000 | 1,500 |
| E. land conservation and rehabilitation | 1,700 | 250 |
| F. water | 5,000 | 800 |
| G. plant genetic resources | - | - |
| H. animal genetic resources | 600 | 300 |
| I.  pest management and control | 200 | 100 |
| J.  plant nutrition | 1,900 | 285 |
| K. energy transition | 3,200 | 475 |
| L. UV radiation | 1,800 | 265 |
| **15. Conservation of biological diversity** | 3,500 | 1,750 |

| Chapter / Programme Area | Total cost for developing countries (US$m/yr) | incl. grant or concessional requirement (US$m/yr) |
|---|---|---|
| **16. Biotechnology** | | |
| A. food and raw materials | 5,000 | 50 |
| B. human health | 14,000 | 130 |
| C. environmental protection | 1,000 | 10 |
| D. safety and international cooperation | | 2 |
| E. mechanisms for development and application | | 5 |
| **17. Protection of oceans** | | |
| A. coastal areas | 6,000 | 50 |
| B. marine environmental protection | | 200 |
| C. marine living resources of high seas | | 12 |
| D. marine living resources in Exclusive Economic Zone (EEZ) | 6,000 | 60 |
| E. climate change | 750 | 480 |
| F. international cooperation | | 50 |
| G. small islands | 130 | 50 |
| **18. Freshwater** | | |
| A. integrated water resources development | | 115 |
| B. water resources assessment | 355 | 145 |
| C. water resources protection | 1,000 | 340 |
| D. drinking water | 20,000 | 7,400 |
| E. urban water | 20,000 | 4,500 |
| F. rural water | 13,200 | 4,500 |
| G. climate change | 100 | 40 |
| **19. Toxic chemicals** | | |
| A. international risk assessment | | 30 |
| B. classification and labelling | | 3 |
| C. information exchange | | 10 |
| D. risk reduction programmes | | 4, incl. A, E. |
| E. national capacities | 600 | 150 |
| F. illegal international traffic | - | |
| **20. Hazardous wastes** | | |
| A. prevention and minimisation | | 750 |
| B. institutional capacities | global 18,500; developing countries 3,500 | 500 |
| C. international cooperation | (no estimate | available) |
| D. illegal international traffic | - | - |
| **21. Solid wastes** | 1%　municipal waste expenditure 1,800 | |
| A. minimisation | | |

| Chapter / Programme Area | Total cost for developing countries (US$m/yr) | incl. grant or concessional requirement (US$m/yr) |
|---|---|---|
| B. recycling | 15,000 | 850 |
| C. disposal and treatment | 7,500 | 3,400 |
| D. extended coverage | | 2,600 |
| **22. Radioactive wastes** | | 8 |
| **24. Women** | | 40 |
| **25. Children and youth** | | |
| A. youth | | 1.5 |
| B. children | | incl. in other programmes |
| **26. Indigenous people** | | 3 |
| **27. NGOs** | relatively limited but unpredictable | |
| **28. Local authorities** | | 1 |
| **29. Trade unions** | | 300 |
| **30. Business and industry** | not expected to be significant | |
| **31. Scientific and technological community** | | 15 |
| **32. Farmers** | in Ch. 14, relevant also Ch. 3, 12, 13 | |
| **34. Technology transfer** | | 450 - 600 |
| **35. Science** | | |
| A. scientific basis | 150 | 30 |
| B. scientific understanding | 2,000 | 1,500 |
| C. long-term scientific assessment | 35 | 18 |
| D. capacity and capability | 750 | 470 |
| **36. Education, public awareness and training** | | |
| A. education | 8,000 - 9,000 | 3,500 - 4,500 |
| B. public awareness | 1,200 | 110 |
| C. training | 5,000 | 2,000 |
| **37. Capacity building** | | 300 - 1,000 |
| **40. Information for decision making** | | |
| A. data gap | | 1,900 |
| B. information availability | | 165 |

**Source:** *Compiled by M. Koch from Agenda 21 text. Chapters 1, 23, 33, 38 and 39 do not contain specific programme areas or associated cost estimates.*

The Secretariat also estimated the fraction of the total resources which would be required from international sources on a grant or concessional basis. Again these were based on rather general principles, for example explicit anti-poverty and population measures receive a high degree of international support (taken at 50% in the Secretariat estimates), whilst infrastructure expenditures on construction etc., and areas like coastal resource management, have a very low international contribution. In some areas (such as the measures for energy under 'atmosphere') only the additional costs associated with environmental measures were included, and ascribed fully to international finance.

The estimates are thus of varied quality and cannot be considered robust. They do however provide at minimum a reasonably systematic starting point for thinking about financial requirements, both in total and its distribution among different activities. The overall impression is to underline perceptions on the scale of money involved: the total annual requirements throughout the 1990s were stated to be $600bn/yr, with $125bn/yr required in grants or concessional loans.[2] This figure is more than twice the current total disbursements of Official Development Assistance (ODA) from developed to developing countries.[3] Coincidentally, it is also close to the official UN target for ODA of 0.7% of GNP from rich countries. To this extent, the financial estimates in Agenda 21 start to identify what this target contribution might be used for.

---

[2] These are very rounded figures. Adding the estimates in Table 1 suggests a total somewhat under $600nbn/yr, with grant or concessional requirements exceeding $130bn/yr.

[3] Official Development Assistance from OECD countries rose from $52,960m in 1990, to $56,709 in 1991 (or $54,730 at 1990 prices and exchange rates). Source: Development Assistance Committee, OECD, Paris. In addition there were private flows of around $55b, about half of which was foreign direct investment.

These need to be placed in the context of international debt. An OECD report *Financing and External Debt in Developing Countries* concludes:

- in 1991 Third World financing exceeded the 1990 record level.

- the overall debt problem has not been solved. There has been considerable improvement in some countries but the situation remains critical in many others.

- the Club of Paris policy of offering an agreement on a country's entire debt (cancelling in practice at least half the debt) in exchange for an adjustment programme is positive and fundamental;

- debt service fell in 1991 ($150.9bn) from 1990 ($159.1bn) and the funds transferred to developing countries increased from $137.2bn in 1990 to $137.5bn in 1991. These figures also show that developing countries continue to pay more than they receive.

Source: As reported in *Europe*, 14/15 September 1992, No.5814.

### Likely resources: UNCED pledges

The UNCED agreements clarified the GEF as the interim funding mechanism for the Conventions, and Agenda 21 stated that the GEF's 'grant and concessional funding is designed to achieve global environmental benefits [and thus] should cover the agreed incremental costs of relevant activities under Agenda 21.'.. At the time of writing the funding actually available to the GEF is unclear. Figures of up to $10bn for the next three-year phase had been widely touted, but few governments announced specific figures concerning GEF funding. Those that did included:

- UK: commitment to play its part in the replenishment of the GEF to the tune of about US$2bn. This works out to about $100m for the UK.
- Germany: commitment to play its part in the replenishment of the GEF to the tune of about US$2-$3bn.

These statements indicate not only lower expectations for the replenishment, but also place greater weight on the need for other countries to 'play their part', unlike the unilateral contributions in the pilot phase (it is also not certain that such figures represent 'new and additional' funding). Commitments will clearly depend to some extent on the outcome of debates on restructuring the GEF (see section 4.7); but given the above the overall level seems unlikely to exceed $1bn/yr for the next three-year phase. Before UNCED, the USA also put up $25m for developing country studies under the FCCC climate convention to be disbursed bilaterally.

To support the more general local and regional environmental concerns, Agenda 21 (33.15) stated that:

'In general, the financing for the implementation of Agenda 21 will come from a country's own public and private sectors. For developing countries, particularly the least developed countries, ODA is a main source of external funding, and substantial new and additional funding for sustainable development and implementation of Agenda 21 will be required. Developed countries reaffirm their commitments to reach the accepted United Nations target of 0.7 per cent of GNP for ODA'.

As noted (sections 4.2, 4.7) developing countries had argued for a separate 'Green Fund', but this was modified in the end to discussion of an 'Earth Increment' in the forthcoming round of International Development Association donations of ODA (IDA-10, agreed in late 1992 - see below)[4]. At UNCED, the President of the World Bank suggested an Earth Increment of around $5bn. However, explicit references to this (or any other) figure was dropped from Agenda 21; it was reported that:[5]

'Some governments are concerned that if UNCED commits to levels for the IDA-10 replenishment it will limit or foreclose options within the ongoing negotiations in other fora. Others believe that it is unrealistic to set funding levels before reviewing the projects that IDA-10 would fund'.

Few specific national figures for commitments of funds for Agenda 21 programmes were mentioned at Rio. Apart from the GEF declarations noted above, Japan led the field with a declaration that environment related ODA for its next five-year cycle would be in the range of $7-7.7bn.

One persistent issue is the difficulty of disguishing environment-related expenditure from other ODA, especially when much of the money is going through bilateral efforts or regional development banks. However, some governments announced specific funding for specific purposes, notably:

- US: US$150m for protection of forests
- Canada: US$113m for protection of forests

Again however it was unclear the extent to which these numbers really represented new and additional money, or how they are to be disbursed, or for what in detail. After UNCED, the Secretariat was of the opinion that it has had no **pledges** of money: government ministers can state figures but these have to be ratified by their own governments and therefore are not considered as pledges.

## Likely resources: outcome and prospects

Recession and related economic problems affecting the richer countries influenced the debate in June, and continue to do so. Norway, one of the world's highest donors in percentage terms, cut its own ODA funding to 1.2% of GNP.

---

[4] The International Development Association (IDA) is the window of the World Bank that poor countries can apply to for funds on a non-commercial basis (ie lower rates of interest). Somewhat under 10% of total ODA goes through the IDA.

[5] *Earth Summit Bulletin*, Vol.2, No.11, Island Press and the International Institute for Sustainable Development, Rio de Janeiro, 13 June 1992.

There was political outcry over suggestions that the UK might actually cut its ODA funding by £200m (15%), and that the EC as a whole might also cut its contribution; in the event, the EC Council reaffirmed that the EC would 'increase funding for Agenda 21 .. to 3 billion ECUs, including new and additional resources for specific projects and programmes in key Agenda 21 sectors .. as an initial contribution ... provide an initial tranche of 600 million ECU in the first year'.[6]

The IDA-10 replenishment, completed in December 1992, saw no 'Earth Increment' of the kind proposed at Rio by the President of the World Bank; the amount finally agreed, resulting in about $16bn available funds over the next 3 year period, represents little, if any, real increase in IDA funds.

Development analysts at the OECD's Development Assistance Committee expect real increases from Japan and some northern European countries, notably those (like France) that have set relatively firm medium-term targets; reports indicate expectations that Japan will increase its total outlay of ODA for the next five-year cycle to more than $70bn over the period. The UNCED declaration suggests that about a tenth of this would be considered additional money for environmental goals. Prospects for the USA and Germany are uncertain; other calls on their money, notably those in Eastern Europe and the CIS, have diminished the prospects. Commenting upon funding in the aftermath of Rio, the president of the World Bank was reported as 'despondent and angry' at the 'failure of industrialised countries to live up to their promises'.[7]

In recent years, the ratio of aggregate ODA to GNP from developed countries has shown remarkable stability at 0.34 (being reduced most notably by the US figure of about 0.2). Continuing recession in the richer countries, competing pressures from the 'transition economies', and other factors mean there is a prospect that the real level may start to decline, rather than increase. The only additional money made available may therefore be limited to other bilateral funds, private finance, and the amounts provided to establish the CSD and strengthen the key UN institutions of UNEP and the UNDP. Whatever the final outcome, the amount of additional money available will clearly be pitifully small compared even against the numbers discussed in the run-up to Rio, and quite negligible in comparison with the requirements crudely estimated by the UNCED Secretariat.

---

[6] CEC Press Release, 1083/92 (Presse 211), 18 November 1992, CEC, Brussels. 1ECU = US$1.2.

[7] *Financial Times*, 25 September 1992.

## Appendix 2

### Sources of further information

This book has reproduced only the most important parts of the texts from the UNCED agreements, and supporting material and events are only referenced where directly relevant.

The full text of the two Conventions will appear in international legal sources, such as *International Legal Materials*, and the *International Environmental Reporter* published by the Bureau of National Affairs, Washington DC. The full texts of all the UNCED agreements are available from the UN Publications Office (Room DC2-0853, Dept 9211, UN, New York 10017), and from the UNCED Secretariat Offices:

New York: Room S-3060, United Nations, New York 10017.
Tel: +(1-212)-963-5959; Fax: +(1-212-963-1010).
Geneva: 160 Route de Florissant, P.O. Box 80, CH-1231 Conches, Geneva, Switzerland.
Tel: +(41-22)-789-1676; Fax: +(41-22)-789-3536;

The texts are also available on computer diskette from:

The Centre For Our Common Future, Palais Wilson, 52 Rue des Paquis, CH-1201 Geneva. Tel: +(41-22)-732-7171 Fax: +(41-22)-738-5046. Email gn:commonfuture.

Publications from the Centre for Our Common Future also provide one of the main published avenues for information on international developments in the area.

The International Union for the Conservation of Nature and Oceana Publications are preparing a comprehensive compendium and analysis of the UNCED agreements, which is projected at the time of writing to comprise six volumes (Oceana Publications Inc, 75 Main Street, Dobbs Ferry, NY 10522).

The official UNCED texts have also been published in 'The Earth Summit', Graham and Trotman/Martin Nijhoff, London/Dordrecht/ Boston, 1993.

About 130 governments produced national reports to UNCED before the conference. As well as generally being available from the relevant Departments in the countries concerned, they are being published in three volumes by the UN as the 'Nations of the Earth Reports', available from the UN Publications Office.

As noted in Section 2.5, during the UNCED process and at the Global Forum, disparate non-governmental environment and development groups sought to negotiate 'alternative treaties' to indicate what they would like to have seen. About forty were initiated[1]. Of these, 29 completed agreements are published in *The Rio Treaties of the Global NGO Movement*, Adamantine Press. 3 Henrietta Street, London WC2E 8LU.

The International Institute for Applied Systems Analysis (IIASA) in Vienna is coordinating a major project on the Process of International Negotiations, which will include a detailed study of UNCED and surrounding events. Details are available from IIASA, Schlossplatz 1, A-2361, Laxenburg, Austria.

Information on the Earth Council, established immediately after UNCED, is available from the Earth Council Organising Committee, PO Box 323-1001 San Jose, Costa Rica. E-mail: abarcena@igc.apc.org.

For anyone equipped with a computer and modem the most comprehensive and flexible sources of information are the various electronic conferences on the Econet computer network. As well as the full text of the official documents, the Econet system gathers much of the commentary material on UNCED and the Conventions. These include the Earth Summit Bulletin, which reported daily on PrepCom and UNGA negotiations whilst they were in progress and on subsequent developments, and other bulletins attending convention negotiations. Also posted on Econet are the non-governmental 'alternative treaties' negotiated among NGOs for Rio.

Econet within the USA is managed by the Institute for Global Communications, 3228 Sacramento Street, San Francisco, CA 94115, (415)-442-0229). Outside the US, access is via the network of the Association for Progressive Communications, based at Alternex-IBASE, Rua Vicentre de Souza 29, 22251 Rio de Janeiro, Brazil. Most countries have local branches, or networks connected directly to APC. The UNCED documents are also to become available through the Earth Sciences network CIESIN.

The management of information in a process as broad as UNCED, and the networks which developed to enable rapid global communications, could doubtless form a study in their own right.

---

[1]A summary of the major agreements is given in Ecoforum, Vol.16, No.2, 1992 (ELCI, Nairobi, Kenya)